Easy Peasy

DOGGY

Squeezy

EVEN MORE OF YOUR DOG TRAINING DILEMMAS SOLVED

Easy Peasy

DOGGY

Squeezy

STEVE MANN

& Martin Roach

BLINK
bringing you closer

First published in the UK by Blink Publishing
An imprint of Bonnier Books UK
Wimpole Street, London, W1G 9RE
Owned by Bonnier Books
Sveavägen 56, Stockholm, Sweden

facebook.com/blinkpublishing
twitter.com/blinkpublishing

Trade Paperback – 978-1788703-41-3
Ebook – 978-1788703-42-0

A CIP catalogue of this book is available from the British Library.

Typeset by Envy Design Ltd
All Photographs © Dan Rouse
All illustrations © Shutterstock
Printed and bound in Great Britain by Clays Ltd, Elcograf S.p.A.

1 3 5 7 9 10 8 6 4 2

This book is not intended to be a substitute for Veterinary advice. If you are concerned that your dog has a behavioural or other disorder, you should seek Veterinary advice. The author and publisher will not be liable for any loss or damage in connection with or arising out of the performance or use of methods described and contained in this book.

Every reasonable effort has been made to trace copyright holders of material reproduced in this book, but if any have been inadvertently overlooked the publishers would be glad to hear from them.

Blink Publishing is an imprint of Bonnier Books UK
www.bonnierbooks.co.uk

For my dad, who never entered a room without a silly song, and for my mum, who told me to do the job that makes me the happiest.

ABOUT THE AUTHOR

For over 30 years, Steve Mann has been a professional dog trainer and has worked with over 100,000 dogs and owners worldwide. He is the author of the bestselling book, *Easy Peasy Puppy Squeezy* and is also Chairman of the Institute of Modern Dog Trainers. This organisation has education centres for dog trainers and behaviourists throughout the UK, Australia, South Africa and China. He is a regular speaker at dog training and behaviour events around the world, including conferences in South Africa, the Middle East and throughout Europe. Steve has also trained many dogs, owners and handlers within the pet, detection and security world, has a long list of celebrity clients and appears on TV, radio and other media to demonstrate and promote the value of positive dog training.

He lives in Hertfordshire with his family, many rescue dogs, horses, chickens and a goose called Gandalf.

CONTENTS

PART 4:

LEARNING ABOUT DOGS, LEARNING ABOUT TRAINING

INTRODUCTION

THANK YOU SO MUCH FOR PICKING UP THIS COPY OF *EASY PEASY DOGGY SQUEEZY* – I'M GUESSING YOU'RE A DOG NUT, TOO!

I'm really excited for you that you're going to find lots of answers to your dog training questions here. Living with a dog can be a wonderful life-affirming experience; however, it can also be a real pain in the butt, so my role is to offer exercises and solutions to simply make life better *for you both.*

As a lifelong trainer and founder of the Institute of Modern Dog Trainers, the largest education and membership body for trainers and behaviourists worldwide, I get asked A LOT of 'dog' questions! Many of these queries are frequently repeated and it's those questions, and importantly those answers, that I've distilled for you here, so I'm sure there's plenty for you to get stuck in to. I haven't published the answers to the simplest questions, and likewise I haven't explained the answers to the most complicated (however, Mrs Jenkins from Poole, if you're reading this, dogs should NEVER wear roller skates!).

What I have done is split the book into four sections:

🐾 *Important Exercises To Teach Your Dog*

🐾 *Problem Behaviours and How to Help*

🐾 *Exercises for Quality of Life*

🐾 *Learning About Dogs, Learning About Training*

Not only am I a dog nut, but I'm also a dog *training* nut, so it's important to me that I don't just tell you what to do and how to do it, but also *why*. My job is to get across why we're teaching an exercise and, importantly, *why* we're teaching it that particular way. If we understand the 'why' of a behaviour – the 'benefit' – we're much more likely to put it into practice.

When I'm teaching, I always imagine the students are saying to themselves, *Yeah, but why, what's in it for me?'* and that's fair enough. To that end, when you're asking your dog to do a behaviour, it's only fair that you realise they're asking the same question!

Please read these letters in the order of the book – no flicking allowed! The reason being that these exercises have been deliberately structured in this order because what you learn in the earlier exercises, you can then apply to the later ones.

Remember, dogs are always a work in progress and in my experience you and your dog's standard of training will never stand still – it will either go backwards or it'll go forwards ... your choice!

I'm a dog trainer by trade and teaching is my passion, but it's the love of my own dogs that has inspired me to write this book. What I explain here aren't only the methods I use to help owners and dogs professionally, but also the skills that have helped me live with the dogs I've owned and loved throughout my life. It's those skills that I want to share with you now, so you too can make the most of your lives together.

Settle in, have a read, make notes, reflect, make a plan, look at the world from your dog's perspective and get to work! Enjoy the process and, above all else, be friends.

Steve Mann

THE ACTIVE INGREDIENTS

B ig or small, yappy or quiet, all shapes and sizes ... and that's just the owners! Throw all of our individual dogs into the mix, with their different personalities, characters, loves and dislikes, and it's easy to see that in dog training, no one size fits all.

There are so many variables in dog training to consider. Even in my own career I've gone from being buried in snow as a 'decoy', waiting hours for the Search and Rescue dogs to *pleeease* find me, to working with rescued Pit Bulls in South Africa; puppy classes in Australia; detection dogs in the Middle East; and in and out of thousands of households in England and Ireland helping owners with their own very individual dogs, each with their own very individual problems.

What we need is to create a bespoke solution for your

dog and your circumstances. The way you'll do that is not to look for one-off recipes or solutions, but to focus on what I like to call...

THE SEVEN ACTIVE INGREDIENTS

We will visit these Seven Active Ingredients time and time again throughout this book. Understand and apply these ingredients to any behaviour you want more of, or indeed any behaviour you want less of, and you'll be on the right track to a happier life with your dog!

Active Ingredient One: Reinforcement
Reinforcement occurs as a *consequence* to a behaviour and makes that behaviour more likely to occur in the future. Put simply, if you ask your dog to do something, make sure you pay them well!

Active Ingredient Two: Mutually Exclusive Behaviours (known as MEBs)
I'm not in the business of telling the dog what *not* to do, I'm in the business of reinforcing the behaviours I *do* want instead.

A Mutually Exclusive Behaviour (MEB) is simply a behaviour that while the dog is doing it, they physically can't also be doing the unwanted behaviour *at the same time*. A classic example would be if your dog jumps up to you to say 'Hello', we're going to heavily treat your dog for *sitting* when you arrive. Your dog can't jump up at you when their butt is on the ground!

Active Ingredient Three: Associations

How a dog *feels* is far more important than what a dog *does*.

Now, I appreciate that may not seem the case when you're holding onto a lamp-post to try and stop your dog from barking and lunging at another dog! However, that unwanted behaviour may be occurring because your dog has a negative association to the presence of other dogs. By changing the association, which changes how the dog FEELS, we'll change the behaviour. We'll teach your dog to feel good about the presence of other dogs and if we understand the ingredients, we can also help with the presence of postmen, kids and, who knows, maybe even cats!

Active Ingredient Four: Control and Management

The first rule of any training programme is to not let the unwanted behaviour occur and get reinforced. That's why Control and Management (C&M) is so important.

We don't want to try to run before we can walk, so it's important that we don't put the dog in a position of being reinforced somehow by doing unwanted behaviours. If you call your dog and *they don't come to you*, we don't want them to be inadvertently *reinforced* by then running off to play with other dogs. In this instance, good C&M will

be a long line attached to their harness so you can stay in contact.

If your dog gets a *reinforcing* cuddle when jumping up at 'untrained' visitors at the door, then good C&M dictates that you pop your dog in the kitchen before opening the door.

Good, reliable training takes a little bit of time to spin the wheels before you get any traction, but C&M works instantly. **Don't see C&M as avoiding the problem, see it as *stopping the problem occurring.***

Active Ingredient Five: Cues

'Cues' are simply what triggers a behaviour from your dog:

- 🐾 'STOP!' cues *'Freeze no matter what'* (if you've read this book).

- 🐾 'COME!' cues *'Run to the monkey for good times'* (if you've read this book).

- 🐾 'DING DONG!' at the front door cues *'Oh my God! EMERGENCY! EMERGENCY! SCREAM! MURDERER!'* (if you've not yet read this book).

Active Ingredient Six: The 3-Ds

It's one thing to call your dog from five metres, but from 50 metres? Sure, you may be able to ask your dog to sit quietly in front of you, but can they sit quietly in front of a child who is messily eating an ice cream?

We're going to teach our dogs a lot of behaviours, on cue. At first, we'll set a nice low achievable bar so your dog can hit the desired criteria to earn reinforcement.

Once *established*, we can raise the bar by increasing what I call 'the 3-Ds':

Distance

If your dog learns a fantastic 'Emergency Stop' at 10 metres, then sneak away and see if you can reinforce a stop at 20 metres. All good? Cool, try 30 metres.

Duration

Perhaps your dog is doing a lovely 'Down' as soon as you ask for the behaviour. Next, you would focus on getting a down for five seconds, then 10 seconds and so on.

Distraction

If your dog is brilliant with their 'Sit', then ask them to do so while you jump up and down or bend over to tie up your shoe laces, or whatever distraction you can think of. (Perhaps you have access to a trombone?!)

We will come across the 3-Ds in more specific applications throughout the book, but here's a small word of caution before we start: don't constantly raise and raise and raise the criteria every time. There's no need for such pressure on either of you. Even Usain Bolt isn't expected to do a personal best every time he runs!

Active Ingredient Seven: Proofing

Anyone can teach their dog to do a 'Recall' from the garden, or a 'Sit' by the fridge in the kitchen, but can they get the same reliable behaviours in the park or at the vets? To ensure your training is as reliable as possible: first teach in one location, then *proof* the behaviours by reinforcing them in a variety of locations, times of day and weather conditions.

These Seven Active Ingredients are your 'tools of the trade' to help you and your dog negotiate any training or behavioural issues. This book will help you master them so you'll be able to come up with as many different solutions as you fancy to either help your dog *do a behaviour you want*, or to encourage them to *do an alternative behaviour to the ones you don't want.*

As you read through *Easy Peasy Doggy Squeezy*, you'll see how we thread many of the ingredients throughout our recipes. We won't use all of them for every issue but by understanding and applying them correctly, not only can we can train with compassion and science on our side, but also our dogs will love us all the more for it!

PART 1
IMPORTANT EXERCISES TO TEACH YOUR DOG

Granted, this is the kind of title you'd expect in any typical dog training book, but I believe that the exercises suggested aren't so typical. I want to introduce you to exercises that will offer a real tangible benefit to your lives together, exercises that will make all other exercises easier, or even redundant.

Above all else, an understanding of canine body language makes everything clearer, so I've kicked off with that before we get into the fundamental exercise of 'Focus' – and then move through the daily essentials of 'Down', 'Recall' and 'Loose Lead Walking', before heading into the more elegant, yet functional, exercises of: 'Chin Rest', 'Collar Grabs', 'Reflex to Name' and finally a real crowd-pleaser, the 'Emergency Stop'.

Each exercise has a natural path for you to work through from beginner to advanced, but don't make the mistake of rushing through to get to the more rock 'n' roll *advanced* exercises.

More often than not, *advanced* is simply the *basics* done well!

BODY LANGUAGE

Hello Steve,

We're welcoming a new rescue female Boxer, Ringo (don't ask!), into our home soon and although all reports from the rescue centre are that she's great with dogs, I'm worried she may get into trouble if I let her play with other dogs at my local park. I've been told Boxers can sometimes get picked on by other dogs. What can I look out for to make sure she doesn't get into a scrap?

Lydia

Hi Lydia,

One of the most important skills we can learn to make living with our dogs as valuable and stress-free as possible is for us to become canine body language experts! Boxers can sometimes be a tough read for other dogs due to their somewhat bolshie-looking silhouette: consider the bottom jaw jutting forward aggressively below the furrowed brow, coupled with the broad, inflated chest and it's soon easy to appreciate that an unknown Boxer entering a new park can be seen by some dogs as the equivalent to a guy kicking down the door of a pub, dressed in a Union Jack sleeveless shirt and declaring, 'Who wants it then!?' Throw in the fact that in the past many Boxers had their tails docked, therefore limiting their ability to transmit friendly intentions, and it's understandable that Boxers often had one arm tied behind their back when trying to make new friends.

The good news is, I'm obsessed with dog body language! I've dedicated many years and travelled thousands of miles to study dog body language: from the countless pet dogs I've trained, through to the street dogs of Peru, the township dogs of Johannesburg, the beach dogs of Portugal, the desert dogs of Bahrain and everything else in between. One thing I can tell you about dogs and their body language is this: they don't lie!

We monkeys mask a lot of our true feelings with diverting words, ego, sarcasm and bravado. With dogs – and this is why I love them – what you see is what you get. Our duty and responsibility as dog owners is to constantly 'listen', and respond appropriately to what dogs are communicating. This communication doesn't happen when someone 'speaks', it starts when someone *listens*. Take comfort that the rescue centre has said Ringo is great with other dogs. Continue with nice, friendly introductions to steady, confident and friendly dogs and have a little read of the tips below so you can start to become as fluent as possible in 'how to speak dog'...

DOG-TO-DOG COMMUNICATION

Before dogs even get next to each other to play, there's a ton of information we can glean from the way in which they approach each other.

A friendly approach with good intentions will be in the form of a crescent as opposed to a straight-line approach. Watch two friendly people approach to introduce themselves: they'll have nice loose spines, not so much that they'll *jellyfish* their way over to each other on the floor, but there'll certainly be a looseness in the hips. The approach from each will be in a slight crescent; as they meet they'll turn and dip one shoulder to shake hands and their head will tilt to one side. As they stand, their feet will be at 'ten to two', there'll be a bend in the knee, which in turn will put the hips, shoulders and head off-centre. Genuinely friendly people have a lot of flexibility in their bodies when they say 'Hi'. Only an alien shakes hands front-on with square shoulders and no flexibility in their spine (see 'Donald Trump').

If your dog is using this crescent approach towards another dog, that is a great sign. The time to be wary is when we see the opposite in a dog-to-dog approach. What we don't want to see is:

- Direct eye contact with no blinking or eye diversion at least every two seconds

- A straight, stiff spine

- A tightly closed mouth

- A fast, direct head-on approach.

All of these are warning flags and often result in animosity.

Once two dogs with friendly intentions have met, the first thing they do is sniff butts. The crescent approach will put them in the right position to do exactly that. *Face to butt* is a friendlier way for your dog to meet a new dog as opposed to *face to face*. We shake hands, they sniff butts. Be grateful for small mercies!

At this point they will generally sidle backwards and stand cheek to cheek, one of them may do a little sharp, 'C'mon' head flick to the side – you know, the kind of desperate 'Let's go!' gesture you do to your partner at the house party behind the host's back! That head flick is a way to induce a game of 'chase me', often followed by a play bow – 'scary' front end down low, friendly butt end up high. Once committed, both dogs will run off together, ideally with an exaggerated 'rocking horse' stride. It's all very energy inefficient, like two lambs gambolling over a meadow with high front ends and high back ends. This is the polar opposite to the focused, stalking, flat spine that dogs use to hide against the horizon when they're hunting with the intention to bite. The more rocking-horse the dogs' movements are, the clearer it is that the intention of the chase is a friendly one. Good news.

Once the dogs are up and playing, we want to see a nice, loose, relaxed mouth. A good clue is when you can see the bottom teeth, that way you've a good indicator that the dog is relaxed and not in a fighting or hunting mode.

As they run, you want to see moments of them parallel to each other, leaning in, shoulder to shoulder, or butt-barging to induce friendly reactions. When dogs are playing, from an evolutionary point of view, they're essentially practising skills to become more efficient in reproduction, running from danger, hunting, fighting or killing. All pretty hardcore activities, so we need these signals such as rocking horse movements, play bows and butt-barging to remind the receiver, 'I'm only kidding!'

Regardless of age, breed, sex, size and health, it's important that the two dogs take it in turns: one's the chaser, the other's the chasee. Then 60 seconds later, the roles are reversed – the dog that was on top is now lying on their back and the other one is taking the higher ground, even if the two protagonists are a Chihuahua and a Staffordshire Bull Terrier (as is often the case in my household). It's important that the larger dog self-handicaps to ensure there's a fairness and ebb and flow to the game, even if the larger dog hams it up with a pathetic, 'Oh look, I've fallen' as the smaller dog seizes his chance, mouths his 'opponent's' neck and mutters, 'Yeah, who's the Daddy now?!'

When one dog is on their back and the other one is on top, it's important that the dog above is not actually *pinning* the lower dog. You want to be able to see daylight between them; if the one on the bottom wanted to get up, you should be confident that they'd be able to do so without too much of a struggle.

Any vocalisation during this friendly play should be a more drawn-out cartoonish *raaaar raaar raaaar* mouth-wrestling sound, as opposed to a higher-pitched, gull-like back-of-the-throat, sharper vocalisation which suggests frustration and a little bit of temper sneaking into the game. You know when you were play-fighting with your cousin (not now, that'd be weird ... when you were kids), and as you sparred, they made 'Arrrgh, getttt offffff!' sounds, while smiling and attempting to wrestle their way up? Then your knees started to dig into their biceps and your spit-dribble fell onto their face! All of a sudden their movements would get urgent and their voice become higher pitched, louder and more staccato: 'GET! OFF!

SERIOUSLY! NOW!' That's the same with dogs. Without the spit. They're not animals.

Imagine if 'friendly playing' escalating to 'actual conflict' could be measured on a scale of one to ten. Level One being a butt sniff, Level Ten being a fight. Perhaps a play bow is a Level Two, then, as we progress, we see a game of chase easing up the charts into a Level Four and then, straight in at Level Five, a mounting or one dog 'pulling' the other to the ground. Once elements equivalent to a Seven or Eight are being displayed, we want to be seeing either a role reversal, or the dogs opting to stop their interactions for a breather – a self-induced time-out from each other where they pretend to find a really interesting all-consuming smell on the ground (which they've ignored for the last 10 minutes!) or they wander off to have a wee.

That 'pressure-valve' going off at levels Seven or Eight is a way to stop the play tripping over into a conflict. Like a fountain, it pushes on up through the lower levels but when it reaches a certain height, it spills back around to the bottom. So after a break, arousal levels are reduced and then – *Pow!* – a play bow shape is thrown to announce the start of round two and away they go and play starts again at the lower, less intense levels. Experienced, well-rounded dogs that have been exposed to appropriate canine playmates all of their lives will press this 'release' valve themselves. Look out for this moment, it's a beautifully mature conflict resolution tactic.

As a way for owners to allow their dogs to learn and practise such skills, I always advise my new puppy owners to keep puppy introductions and play to just a minute, then get pup back to you, give them a treat, let them chill, then most importantly let them go back and play again. With enough repetition, they'll learn that coming to you leads to a double-positive: a treat *and* a release for more play. They'll also build up a pattern of play, break, play, break, etc. They'll create their own little pressure-release valve. Over time you can extend the interactions from one minute to two, from two to five and so on, as long as it never threatens to tip over into a conflict – keep watching for the warning signs of stiff bodies or frustrated vocalisation.

In addition to watching and responding to your own dog's body language, the decent thing to do is to also consider what the other dog is 'saying'. It's no good if Ringo is having a wonderful time body slamming another dog if the other playmate is politely saying, 'Please don't'. You know yourself, if polite requests are ignored and the onslaught continues, sooner or later the polite question is going to turn into less of a request and more of a demand ... that's when fights break out. There's no need to get to that point, as long as we pick up on the subtle signs that another dog may be saying, 'No, thank you'. Context is everything when discussing how dogs talk to each other, but signs to look out for that suggest the other dog may not be completely comfortable with an approach from Ringo may be:

- A tongue flick or two from the centre of the mouth, like a snake tasting the air

- Moving to stand behind their owner

- A tucked tail

- Raised hackles on the dog's neck, shoulders or back. Raised hackles (or *piloerection* for the swots out there) don't necessarily mean aggression, but certainly confirm the presence of arousal contracting the muscles, causing the hair to stand away from the body.

Also, consider our own species and how we communicate with our bodies. Would you approach a *stranger* who was staring at you, standing upright with a raised head, exposing their throat, chest out and obvious tension in their body? No?

Neither should Ringo.

Plus, if another dog is on a lead, *there's a reason they're on a lead.* They may not be comfortable with other dogs or people, they may have an injury, the owner may just need some quiet time; whatever the reason, give them the space they're entitled to. 'It's okay, my dog's friendly' is not fair, it's the call of the ignorant.

Sometimes you'll approach another dog and although they superficially appear fairly comfortable, they may do a little *displacement behaviour* to signify they'd appreciate just a little more time before deciding to say 'Hello' or not. A displacement behaviour is a normal behaviour, performed out of context. It's a little like when I was asked a tricky Maths question in front of the class at school, if I wasn't comfortable, before answering, my displacement behaviours were scratching my head, chewing my pencil or swinging back on my chair. Nowadays it's easier if I'm asked a tricky question, I just pretend my phone's ringing!

A dog's displacement behaviour may be to sniff the ground, scratch behind their ear, yawn or even start stretching their front, then back legs like they're limbering up for a race.

Of course, there are other 'in-context' occasions when it makes perfect sense for a dog to display these behaviours. Dogs will often yawn as a communication tool for everyone to 'settle down', or as part of their morning stretching routine – they'll wake up, stretch out their back legs, bow down to stretch their front legs, raise their neck, and then yawn. (REMEMBER: Since 1964 it's illegal for an owner watching their dog go through this routine not to say, *"BiiiiiG Stretch!"*, followed by the obligatory, *"BiiiiiG Yawn!"*)

So there you have it, study Ringo's body language and constantly strive to understand what she's saying and what she needs. Keep her happy and keep her safe.

If I could teach only one skill to dog owners, it'd be how to read and *respond* to canine body language. If we can do that, then we can all make a dog's life with us better, which is what it's all about, isn't it?

FOCUS

Hello Steve,

I want to increase my Beagle Foxie's focus on me. For ages I've been trying to teach him to give me eye contact by pulling a treat up towards my face, but unless there's a treat in my hand to start with, he's just not getting it!

I'm beginning to think he may be a bit of a slow learner!

Paul

Hi Paul,

If you've been doing the same exercise for ages and your dog's still not getting it, I don't think it's the dog who's the slow learner! Teaching 'Focus Through Eye Contact' is THE most important foundation exercise to teach. If your dog's not looking at you, it's a pretty safe bet that they're not listening to you, so as a corridor to everything else, focus through eye contact is definitely the route to take.

I'm nothing if not efficient (lazy), so when I'm training I will always ask myself, *What one exercise will make every other exercise easier?* And 99.9% of the time, the answer is 'Eye Contact'.

If your dog voluntarily checks-in and offers you eye contact, it makes:

Daily exercise easier

Recalls easier

Lead walking easier

Response to all other cues ... easier

Living with your dog ... easier.

I'm not a big fan of *luring* eye contact with a treat as you described because 'a treat in the hand' becomes part of the cue and, as you say, if the treat's not there, then the behaviour will likely be missing too. Plus, ironically, the dog needs to be looking at you in the first place to know you have a treat in your hand. ¯_(ツ)_/¯

It's empowering for Foxie to work from an ethos of, *If in doubt, look up to Paul,* or *If I think there's something in it for me, look up to Paul.* I don't want you to have to give a verbal cue or luring action to try to get eye contact. I want Foxie to make the first move.

Have a crack at the exercises below and, as always, start your training in a nice quiet, familiar environment with no distractions.

EXERCISE 1:

- Drop a treat and, as Foxie picks it up, jog a step or two away from him.
- As soon as he catches up with you and stands still, drop another and jog a couple of steps away from him. Repeat six times...

Now, let's try and get some eye contact **before** the treats arrive...

- The next time he catches up to you and stops, *wait.* You wait until he glances up to you as if to say, 'Go on then, drop another!' then ONLY WHEN THE DOG LOOKS AT YOU, say 'Good', *THEN* drop a treat on the floor and move away for your next repetition.

Build on the above stages by slowly moving with Foxie and saying, 'Good' while treating him each time he glances up to you. This will create focus/ eye contact PLUS the foundations for 'Loose Lead Walking' ... more of which later!

EXERCISE 2:

❧ Sit on the floor with Foxie and have five or six treats in your hand. Close your hand around the treats in a loose fist so Foxie can't get at them, and then hold your arm outstretched away from your body. Here's where Foxie will go through his whole repertoire of trial and error: he'll sniff, lick and paw your hand but stand strong, soldier. *Say nothing, do nothing.* Remember we're looking to empower Foxie here, so let him figure it out and, when he does, you'll be there to give him his proverbial high-five.

❧ Keep your eyes peeled on Foxie's face and *the second he glances up towards your chest or face area* say, 'Good', bring your two hands together and give him the treat. Let him enjoy the treat, wait a second or two, then put your loaded fist out to the side again for another go.

That's the beauty of positive reinforcement: every

repetition is another window of opportunity, what a lovely way to learn!

- After each successful repetition, try and 'shape' the behaviour. So initially you'll reinforce a general glance towards your upper body, after a few successful repetitions of that, then withhold the treat until he looks at your chest; repeat until he is looking above your shoulders, then ultimately your face.

When the behaviour is nice and fluent, and Foxie is getting lost in your eyes as soon as you stretch your arm out, we can then start to change the picture a little, but always keep the same common denominator for him: *if Foxie thinks there's something in it for him, look up at Paul.*

Stick to the same criteria of *eye contact = 'Good' and treat,* but...

- Have the treats in your outstretched left arm, rather than your right...

- Do the exercise seated, standing, slowly walking backwards...

- Do the exercise inside, outside, daytime, night-time...

- Do the exercise in various distracting environments...

With the above two exercises under your belt, next up you can start to reinforce eye contact from Foxie in your more informal day-to-day life and routines in order to make it a real 'go-to' behaviour. He will learn he can gain access to all the good things on the back of eye contact, for example:

- Hand on front door handle = *wait for eye contact* = say 'Good' and open the door to commence your walk.

- Walk to the park on lead = *wait for eye contact* = say 'Good' and unclip lead so Foxie can go play.

- Hand on back door handle = *wait for eye contact* = say 'Good' and open the door so Foxie can go explore the garden.

Just remember, make sure your shifts in criteria are wafer thin and continue to build on success. And also, just to clarify: sometimes an owner will mention that they thought looking directly at a dog is a threatening behaviour. Well there's *looking* and there's **LOOKING!** How you look at your first-born isn't going to be the same way you look at a burglar, or at least I hope not! As well as all the training and day-to-day communication benefits connected with eye contact, it is also a great opportunity to eliminate any confusion for our dogs and to help them realise eye contact

from humans has a positive association and is nothing to be afraid of.

In summary, eye contact (and therefore focus) leads to the keys of the kingdom. In my classes, all the dogs are eye-balling the owners saying, *Go on monkey, give us a cue, I bloody love cues!*

Rather than the old picture of the owner issuing grim *commands* to their dog, our ethos here is handing the reigns over to Foxie. *How can I train Paul to do X, Y or Z? Oh yeah, offer him eye contact!*

Remember Paul, there is no such thing as a slow learner, only slow teachers!

PULLING ON THE LEAD

Hi Steve,

We have a five-year-old Golden Retriever called Goldie who we've had since she was a puppy, and she's always been an absolute nightmare for pulling on the lead! Every day I walk her the mile or so to the park and the pulling is unbearable. I try to keep the lead short so she's next to me but find myself having to constantly say, 'Heel' then yank back on the lead, which helps for a pace or two but then she's off pulling again. I think she'd rather the collar choke her than stop pulling, and I can hear her gasping as she drives ahead on the end of the lead. This happens as soon as the lead gets attached to her collar and we're out of the door, even if we're stood still.

I don't want to keep pulling her back as it's infuriating, but also I don't want to constantly have to dangle food under her nose to bribe her to walk nicely for me. For the sake of her neck and my sanity, HELP!

Rosemary

Ah man, FIVE YEARS you've been living with this but still going to the park every day?! You *martyr!/*lunatic! (*Delete as appropriate)

Don't worry, it's my problem now. Let's get a game plan together for you.

It's really important in all training that we don't try and run before we can walk, so if Goldie isn't giving you attention when she's on the lead and you're both stationary, it's too much of a leap to expect her to do so out on a walk as she's passing a conveyor belt of competing attention-grabbers, like a hungry seal at a sushi bar. First things first, let's get Goldie and you on the same frequency.

Contrary to straining every sinew in your body to try and tighten the lead in an attempt to have Goldie next to you, I want you to treat the pair of you and invest in a nice generous lead, approximately 1.5 metres long. This will immediately allow the lead, and you ... *and* Goldie ... to relax. Having tension on the lead or pulling the dog towards you actually creates an opposition reflex, where the more you pull in one direction, the more Goldie will pull in the other. That's a bad starting point. Having a longer lead will give us more opportunity to create – and therefore reinforce – a slack lead.

As you're doing a bit of retail therapy anyway, for the sake of safety and comfort, please get Goldie a nice, well-fitting harness which she'll wear for her training sessions and ultimately for her walks. She's created a habit of leaning into and pulling against her collar, so we're going to create a new habit of a much more acceptable behaviour for when she's wearing her natty new harness.

Every loose-lead journey starts with a single step, so let's work on the essential foundations and move on from there ...

STATIONARY CHECKING-IN

At the risk of seeming like I am repeating myself (which I am!), to expect Goldie to have focus on you on the move when we haven't yet got it when she is stationary is somewhat putting the cart before the horse. So, we need to make that connection first before we add any movement.

Stand in a nice quiet, teetering-on-boring location with Goldie in her harness and attached to the lead. Stand upright and simply drop a treat on the floor to land right in front of Goldie. As she eats it, drop another and when that one's been scoffed drop another ... repeat several times and then *wait* ... she'll glance to the floor waiting for another magic treat to appear and when it doesn't, she'll raise her head and her eyes will ... follow ... the ... line ... back up ... to where the treats came from; when she eventually glances up towards your body to acknowledge your existence, you say 'Good!' and drop another treat. Wait for her to glance back up to you and the split second she does, say 'Good!' and drop another treat. You're now 'marking' the behaviour of eye contact with a 'Good!' and then reinforcing it by dropping a treat.

Now let's add a little duration. Drop a treat, let Goldie eat it and when she looks back up to you, silently count a couple of seconds of eye contact before you say 'Good!' and reinforce as before. This is a great way to lay a strong 'checking-in' foundation, and when it's nice and fluent, you are ready to take it on the road...

CHECKING-IN ON THE MOVE

Carry on as above in the familiar location you've laid a good foundation in. After a couple of stationary check-ins to get the juices flowing, and with you holding the lead at full length with your two hands together at your belt buckle area, start taking a few tiny pigeon steps backwards. As Goldie follows you, the second she glances to your face say 'Good!'. However, this time, rather than dropping the treat onto the floor (which in the past has allowed her to repeat the behaviour of checking-in with you again), take a treat from your pouch and let her take it directly from your hand next to your leg. Like all of us, Goldie will hang out where the good stuff is. Keep moving in slow, unpredictable directions and every time Goldie offers a glance up to you on the move say 'Good', and try to reinforce on the move.

Too often in dog training we only give the reinforcement when we're stationary and if we're not careful the dog learns that if you're not stationary, all bets are off! That can actually go against the principle we're trying to establish here: we want Goldie to believe that if she's in her harness and the pair of you are *on the move together*, it's in her interest to check-in with you. She can't pull and check-in with you at the same time. Everyone's a winner baby, that's no lie!

Make sure you only move your hand to get the treat *after* the appropriate behaviour has occurred and *after* you say 'Good!' It's very important that the lesson for Goldie isn't that *the hand moving to the treat pouch makes food appear* but rather, *when I'm in my harness and offer a check-in to the monkey, food appears.* That way Goldie knows what behaviour gets reinforced and therefore what behaviour she can offer again in the future.

Once this is strong and smooth – remember 'slow is smooth and smooth is fast' – we can then start taking a few more steps in the same direction rather than constantly doing about-turns like a kid spotting a teacher out of school hours.

Start adding more distance of loose lead walking, more duration of checking-in between treats and also change location gradually so you can 'up' the distraction element. A word of warning here: don't do too much and too soon, such that the standard you want to maintain ever deteriorates. If you push your luck too much with the 3-Ds – distraction, duration, distance – at any time the opportunity to reinforce reduces. Don't sweat it, just go back a few steps (metaphorically) to consolidate, and then move on from there. **Training should never feel like a war of attrition. It's not a race, it's far more important to build gradually on success rather than setting yourself up for a fall.**

I agree with you that we don't want to be dangling food in front of Goldie's nose in order to bribe her to walk next to you. That would actually be using the food as a *cue* (which is introduced *before* a behaviour) and not as a reinforcer (which is introduced *after* the behaviour). We don't want to use the food to *cue* the behaviour because Goldie will learn to only do the behaviour *if* she sees the food. We don't want to turn Goldie into a 'show me the money first' kinda dog. So, we'll use the treat as a reinforcer for loose lead walking, never as a cue.

Regarding cues, you mentioned that in the past that when Goldie pulls you say 'Heel' and pull her back. A couple of things to flag up here: a lead makes for a good safety tool but is actually a terrible communication tool for all concerned. I'm sure it's with the best intentions but I guess you've created a fairly vicious circle: Goldie pulls, you say 'Heel', then you pull, Goldie feels pain, then Goldie pulls, you say 'Heel', and on and on until eventually you arrive at the park. Then Goldie is relieved to get away from the discomfort of the tight collar on her neck and you go off to try to get some blood-flow back into your arm!

When we're looking at cues and what they mean, the perspective to start from is always, 'What does it mean to the dog?'

What does 'Heel' mean to Goldie? At the moment, the best-case scenario is:

Goldie pulls as you say 'Heel'.

Goldie pulls again as you say 'Heel'.

What behaviour has 'Heel' been paired and therefore associated with? Pulling! (*I bet you thought it meant the opposite!*)

At the moment, the worst-case scenario is:

You say 'Heel', then yank the lead.

'Heel' isn't being used as a cue.

'Heel' is being used as a threat.

That's not the way to encourage a dog to want to be around you.

Cues can be verbalised, as we usually imagine dog training to be; for example, you say 'Sit', the dog sits. However, cues can also be drawn from the *environment* and in our case, the fact that you've done plenty of foundation work of reinforcing Goldie when she's in her *harness* and *looking at you*, then in future being in her harness and on the move is the *new cue* to let her know that it's in her interest to check-in with you. No need to add a verbal cue or to yank the lead; the harness and correct reinforcement will suffice.

Focusing on reinforcing the good rather than focusing on punishing the bad is so much better for the soul.

The good news is, you won't always have to be reinforcing with the treats, that's just to get us up and running. Ultimately the loose lead walking will be environmentally reinforced by the joy of the walk, the opportunity to experience new smells and the fun of the park, but in terms of the foundation stages of dog training – food is king.

Once you've done all of the groundwork and built a strong reinforcement history for checking-in and loose lead walking, then if Goldie gets a little over-excited and forges ahead on the lead, you can simply stop. No need to pull her back, if you've been generous enough in the past, she'll soon twig what position to get herself back into, so the walk – and the appropriate reinforcement – can continue for her.

Loose lead walking is often cited as a fairly easy exercise to master, but in my experience it's honestly one of the toughest. The reason being, we often expect it before we teach it. I know in the past, walking out of your front door has felt like you're entering the battle in a gladiatorial arena, so look at today as a fresh start.

Build a super-strong foundation by reinforcing the checking-in on the move, and the pair of you will soon be getting the most from your walks AND you get to keep your collarbone. Great success!

CHIN REST

Hi Steve,

Our little Springer Spaniel Rosie recently had a bout of conjunctivitis, which thankfully cleared up with regular eye drops. However, she was a real 'wriggler' when it was time to give her the medication and she would even sometimes disappear the moment she knew the drops were coming! The vet says there's every chance the conjunctivitis may come back, so I just wondered if there was any training I can do in preparation of having to give eye drops again in the future, as I think I've already used up all of my tricks and cunning this time around!

Thanks!

Lucy

Hi Lucy,

Yep, let's get a game plan together for you right away, otherwise you'll be jumping out of various cupboards like a ninja or having to come up with complicated systems involving pulleys and mirrors just to pop a few drops into Rosie's eyes!

We're going to have a two-pronged attack to combat this one:

Change the 'Emotional Association'. At present, Rosie hides when she knows the eye drops are coming. We're going to reverse that negative association, so she grows to love eye drop time. As Rosie currently has a bad association with the eye drops, we want to change that emotional 'picture' as much as possible and to start afresh. I suggest we take the low-hanging fruit first by removing the 'poisoned' elements that have predicted bad news for Rosie in the past.

Change the place where you store the eye drops. If you heading towards the cupboard in the kitchen fills Rosie with dread that the eye drops are about to be produced, then store the eye drop bottle in the hallway drawer instead.

Change what the eye drops look like. If you need to stick with the same brand that's no problem, but I'd like you to change what the bottle looks like; perhaps wrap a blue bandage around it so it looks completely different.

Change what the eye drops smell like. Dogs have such a strong olfactory system they really *can* smell trouble coming a mile away. If you've wrapped a bandage around the bottle, pop a couple of drops of lavender on the cloth. We're going to condition this so that a lavender aroma predicts only good news as far as Rosie is concerned.

Right, we've prepared our tools as much as possible, let's get on with the positive conditioning. If in the past you've given the eye drops in the kitchen, then I want you to start this process from scratch in the living room, so Rosie doesn't carry over any past suspicions.

With Rosie in the living room with you, go to the drawer, take out the bottle, give Rosie a treat, another treat, then put the bottle back.

Repeat several times and each time Rosie sees you take out and hold the bottle, treat, treat, treat, and stop giving the treats when the bottle goes back into the drawer.

That way you're creating a clear relationship that it's *the presence of the bottle* that makes the good stuff happen.

Extend the above process over several sessions by getting the bottle from the drawer, sitting down in your chair, then treat, treat, treat, then stop the treats and return the bottle.

When you see Rosie clearly happy that you're going through the above routine, then you'll know that you're already halfway there to creating a happier eye drop routine.

The second part of the puzzle to work upon is to teach the 'Chin Rest'. We're going to teach Rosie to happily offer her face to you so you can safely pop the eye drops in for her. This is much better than wrestling her to the ground like a rodeo cowboy!

This is a two-pronged attack: we help Rosie feel good about the activity and we reinforce a more appropriate behaviour.

A great chin rest will look like this:

- You sit in your chair

- You offer the palm of your left hand facing upwards between your knees

- You say 'chin' and Rosie happily places her chin on your hand, giving you the ideal opportunity to dispense the drops.

This is how you're going to teach that chin rest:

1. Sit in your chair facing Rosie and feed her 10 treats, one at a time with your right hand as she sits between your knees. Once done, throw a final treat away from you for Rosie to go and get. The reason we feed in position several times first is to make 'sitting between your knees facing you' a real hotspot where Rosie wants to hang out. The

reason you throw a single treat away from you is to enable Rosie to <u>return</u> to the hotspot, therefore volunteering the foundation behaviour and position we want to build on...

2. Once Rosie eats the thrown treat, encourage her back between your knees by showing her the treat in your right hand. This time use the treat to lure her chin over your left hand which will be waiting between your thighs, palm facing upwards. When her chin brushes your left palm as she targets the treat, say 'Good', place the treat in her mouth and then throw the second treat to enable you to reload and repeat...

3. Once the above is nice and fluent, as she returns to you the next time don't have a treat in your right hand, but still use that hand to lure her chin into position over your left palm. Say 'Good' as she does so, then this time take a treat from your pouch, pop it into her mouth and throw a second treat for her to go get, so you can reload and repeat...

4. As above but say the cue, 'Chin' as she targets her chin onto your left palm. Make sure your palm-facing-up left hand is clearly visible and the position is consistent as that will become an important part

of cueing the behaviour. When she's in position, count one second, say 'Good' and reinforce as before, one in the mouth then one thrown to reload ... then repeat, but after each successful repetition, add another second's duration before reinforcing...

5. Once Rosie is reliably resting her chin on your palm when you give the 'Chin' cue, there'll be no more need for you to throw a treat; simply hit your duration target for the chin rest, say 'Good' and pop a treat into Rosie's mouth.

6. To really strengthen the behaviour, start adding a little bit of extra movement and distraction (this will also simulate the actual procedure you'll be looking to perform with the eye drops). So, for example, as Rosie places her chin onto your palm, gently stroke her shoulders, then her head (to add distraction), say 'Good', remove your left hand and reinforce. As you progress, you can get your chin rest, pretend to dispense eye drops with a pretend invisible eye drop bottle (available from my website), say 'Good' and reinforce.

When all of the above is good and solid, then you can introduce the actual, newly positively conditioned eye drop bottle into the picture in place of the pretend invisible eye drop bottle. When you get to the point of actually dispensing real drops into Rosie's eyes, you will have done hundreds of positively associated repetitions that will have lengthened her 'fuse' and increased her tolerance so that as soon as the drops land and you say, 'Good', she'll be over the moon and waiting with a smile for her treat!

I'm convinced that how a dog feels is far more important than what a dog does, so it's really important that you tread lightly and take the whole process above nice and slow. The value is in the preparation and doing all of the repetitions to create a super-strong positive association for all of the elements linked to dispensing eye drops.

As well as the positive association, both confidence for Rosie and trust in you will come from the knowledge that at any point she can simply walk away to say, 'No, thank you'. This is because throwing the second treat away from her is a constant reminder that she has an 'out' if needs be. You need to notice that if she feels the need to bail out, that's just information for you that you've gone too far too soon, it's a nice way for her to let us know. Simply end that session and for the next one, go right back to the basics, consolidate and build up from there.

The chin rest can be used for many different applications including grooming, vet inspection and ear cleaning. If you want to use the chin rest for a task where ideally you'd like to use both hands, such as teeth brushing, then

teach Rosie to target a towel on your lap rather than an upturned palm. Seeing as Rosie is a Springer Spaniel, the chin rest will come in handy during the summer months when you'll spend most of your time removing sticky buds from her fringes!

I love teaching dogs the chin rest as not only can it be conveniently used for so many different applications, but it's also a really good way to add a positive spin to tasks that in the past have been nothing but bad news as far as the dog's concerned.

RECALL

Hi Steve,

I live with my crazy but beautiful 22-month-old English Bull Terrier Marvin who I love dearly. We rescued him from the shelter when he was six months old. He's a super-friendly little chap, so I'd love to be able to let him off the lead and know that he has a reliable recall. Being a Bullie (by name, not nature!), I appreciate some people may be wary of him bowling over to them for cuddles, so a 100% reliable recall would be fab! He loves his tuggie-rope toy and if I'm waving that in my hand, he'll never stray more than five feet from me; however, if it's not in my hand, I'm not so confident!

Over to you!

Yours hopefully,
Laura

Hey Laura,

Good to hear you still love Marvin 'dearly' – I can tell that you do by the fact you know he's exactly 22 months old! I've got mates with children and when they're asked how old the kids are, they say, 'I dunno, 12-13-ish?'

I'm a big fan of Bullies and it's great that you appreciate some people may not necessarily replicate Marvin's 'lust for life' if he bombs towards them all guns blazing to say 'Hello'. First things first, no matter what some people may say, dog trainers included, NO dog has a 100% reliable 'Recall'. While we're at it, consider this: you and I speak the same language, we know exactly what 'Come here' means and I'm *sure* we're above average intelligence and courtesy, but even then, I couldn't *guarantee* you'd come when I called you or vice versa. There's just no such thing as a 100% reliable recall, not even from humans. So, take that pressure of expectation off your shoulders. However, what we can do is tip all the cards in our favour to make Marvin's recall as reliable as possible, given the situation.

You say he loves his tuggie-rope toy? Ace, we'll definitely use that and we'll also use a long line on his harness during training to prevent any mishaps occurring and Marvin becoming an unwelcome visitor to a fellow walker or dog on the lead. As I mentioned earlier, it's never good or fair to let our dogs run up to another dog if the other dog is on a lead – simply because you can bet there's a good reason why they're on the lead: maybe they're not comfortable with other dogs, maybe they've got an injury or maybe they themselves don't have a safe recall nailed down yet. Whatever the reason, if another dog is on the lead, let's give them a swerve.

Right, on to our training plan... What we want to do is 'pair' the cue 'Come!' with Marvin's tuggie-rope. If we're working with a dog that isn't so tuggie-crazy, we can pair the cue with something equally pleasurable such as liver-cake or a ball on a rope. *Remember: it's what 'Come!' means to Marvin that's important here, not what it means to us.*

Start somewhere safe and secure such as your back garden. Don't go out there and immediately start your training session, we don't want to have to compete with the environment, so let Marvin mooch around for a few minutes, splash his boots and satiate himself with any novelty the garden has to offer.

Once there's no fear of distraction, sneak up towards Marvin and when you're next to him, happily say 'Come!', *then* produce the tuggie-rope toy and have the game to end all games, open a whole can of joy into the session for 30 seconds then stop, suddenly, and become quiet and passive again.

Marvin's eyes will be spinning like a buffering computer cursor but you will have started the process of pairing the cue 'Come!' with the idea that great things are going to happen where you are. That's what 'Come!' will mean to

Marvin, '*Great things where you are*'. The running to you – the actual recall – will just be a freebie by-product he'll perform on his way to gather his prize.

Give it a few minutes, then stand next to Marvin and say 'Come!', again produce the tuggie-rope and have another proper high-octane English Bull Terrier-graded game – see it as a part of your daily exercise regime!

After several repetitions of the above, two things will start happening:

1) The neighbours will call the police thinking you've lost the plot ... but more importantly...

2) Marvin will start lurking around you as if to say, 'Go on Laura, say "Come!" again, I love this recall game!'

When you see Marvin hanging around in anticipation, then we have evidence that the conditioning – the pairing of 'Come!' to the game – is beginning to key in. Just make sure you keep the tuggie out of sight from Marvin until you call 'Come!' It's important that he learns it's the sound of 'Come!' that makes the tuggie-rope appear and the games commence.

Repeat the above a few times then put the toy away and end the session.

Next time, pop out into the garden again, let Marvin have his sniff around, let him have a piddle then, when he's not looking at you, walk a few steps away from him and ... 'COME!' and pull out the toy and go bananas! Even if he doesn't look directly at you (He will. Why wouldn't he? You're going bananas, EVERYONE'S looking directly at you!) play, play, play, it's what Marvin lives for, so make sure he learns it follows when you say 'Come!'

We want Marvin's reaction to your recall cue of 'Come!' to be like a reflex. If I poked you in the back, you wouldn't say to yourself, '*Hmm, who's that poking me in the back, I wonder who that is? You know what? I'm gonna turn around and have a look...*' No, you're going to turn around snap-quick, and that's exactly the reaction I want Marvin to have to his recall cue.

You know the way dogs go nuts when they hear the doorbell? Well, you're doing your very own version of that. No one has *intentionally* taught their dogs to get excited and run to the door when the bell goes, but the sound of the bell has been followed enough times with a chemical brain-bath of exciting visitors that with enough repetitions, when the bell chimes, the dogs run *to the location* of the predicted good stuff. Our training sessions are evolving that notion, you say the sound of the cue, 'Come!' and Marvin runs *to the location* of the predicted good stuff – in this case, you and Mr Tuggie.

Once you're confident of Marvin *running* to you 10 times out of 10 for a play each time you call 'Come!' then we can upgrade the environment; we're going to raise the bar and increase the distraction. This is where the long line comes in. I want to you fit the five-metre long line to Marvin's harness and, *if you're in a safe area*, you can just let it drag behind him on the ground. If you have any doubt at all, you can simply hold onto the line as an extra insurance. Perhaps practise in a quiet corner of the park, only steadily going more 'live' with the recalls when you're regularly hitting 10 out of 10 for Marvin running with the speed of a puma to you the split-second he hears, 'Come!'

A word of warning: the investment you're making in the training above is all about teaching Marvin that 'Come!' predicts the *start* of the good times. I've seen too many people put in the early hard yards to teach the above foundations, but once the recall becomes reliable, they tend to take their foot off the gas and mostly just use the recall cue to *end* the good times, i.e. only calling the dog at the end of the walk to put the lead on and go home. *Boo hoo!* That's like me calling my son away from playing football with his mates ... 'Come here! Come On! Over here!' and as he eventually trots towards me and asks 'What?', I say 'Did you tidy your bedroom?' Sod that! He's going to be in no rush the next time I call him, is he?

It's important that you do several positive recalls throughout each walk and each time make sure it's in Marvin's interest to come to you. Your role is to simply confirm to him that he was right to sprint to you when you called.

Your training should always be *fun in the present* and *an investment in the future*. Build up a positive history so if the time ever comes to call Marvin away from danger, the success won't rely on what you have for him in that moment, but what you've had for him in all of those successful recalls in the past.

As Marvin's recall improves and your confidence grows, you can happily relax on your walks knowing that his recall is as reliable as possible.

Don't get complacent because one thing's for sure: recalls *never* stay the same: they'll either improve or they'll deteriorate.

It's up to you!

COLLAR GRABS

Hello Stephen,

Our English Bullmastiff puppy Chad has learned to become very canny at the park by playing 'stay-away' at the end of our daily walk. His recall is fairly decent but at the end of the walk he can be a real pain to get hold of. Thirty minutes of 'stay-away' is his record so far and unless I learn how to use a lasso, I dare say he'll soon beat that time! He's really friendly and the park is fully enclosed so safety here is not a real issue, but the time-wasting and embarrassment is!

Thanks for your help!

Phil

Hello Phil,

'*Stephen*'? Who are you, my mum?!

I love the way you say that Chad 'has learned' to stay away from you at walks. I wonder who taught him that?! As I mentioned in *Easy Peasy Puppy Squeezy*, dogs are always learning, the tricky part is that they're not always learning what we think we're teaching them.

To ensure you're never going to have to resort to trying to throw your coat over Chad to escort him from the park like a rock star leaving a concert, let's teach you both the beauty of a 'Collar Grab'. For a dog that's learned the unwanted skill of playing stay-away, it can be a really important safety exercise. Thankfully your local park is enclosed and gated, but I want you to be safe should Chad ever find himself running around to the theme tune of *Born Free* anywhere else that may not be so secure.

First up, for comfort and safety, I'm a big fan of dogs having the lead attached to a harness rather than a collar, so I'm going to cover the exercises of 'Collar Grabs' and 'Lead to Harness' for you.

TEACHING THE COLLAR GRAB

1. In the evening when you're at home and both chilled, sit on the floor next to Chad with your back against the settee as you stroke him; give it a few moments,

say 'Grab', gently put two fingers under his collar, say 'Good' and give him a treat. Repeat 10 times.

2. Next, do the same again, but when you say 'Good', *throw* the treat so Chad can voluntarily return to you, this is important as unless you have the arms of Mr. Tickle we're going to want to rehearse the all-important *returning to you* aspect of the exercise for it to have any real-life value. Pretty soon Chad will start pushing his collar in towards your hand as he returns so as to say, *'Go on then, give us a grab!'* If so, good news, I always want the dog to believe *they're* training *us*. Repeat 10 times. What you're doing here is reversing the thought process Chad has associated with collar grabs; no longer does the movement predict bad news, such as the end of a walk, but good news ... treats!

3. For this stage, once you've thrown the first treat, sit up on the settee and open your stance a little so Chad can return between your legs to gain his collar grab. This will help create the habit of Chad getting in nice and close to you, and will shatter the invisible magnetic force-field that's kept him the critical *stay-away* distance from you in the past. Say 'Grab' just before you hold his collar. Do several repetitions, the more the merrier, as long as Chad is enjoying the process.

In the past, 'uninvited' hands coming *may* have been signalling to him that something cool was incoming, such as cuddles and food, or *may* have been signalling to him that something not-so-cool was about to happen, such as the lost opportunity to run off to doggy pals or the end of a fun walk. At this stage, and for the rest of eternity, every single time Chad hears the phrase 'Grab', it predicts *only good*. Saying 'Grab' importantly removes *all suspicion* and **the more we can remove suspicion from a dog's life, the more reliable, trusting, predictable and consistent their behaviour will be.**

N.B. Hold the collar THEN go for the treat. Your *hand on the collar* predicts the food is coming, not your *hand in the pouch* – a very important distinction.

As the sessions progress, keep the common denominators of:

'Grab' + collar hold = 'Good' + treat ... but add some more real-life variables, such as:

- 🐾 Angle of approach, left-hand collar grab, right-hand collar grab, grab from above, grab from below...

- 🐾 Do it with you in a sitting, standing and lying (!) position.

- 🐾 Vary the tension, speed of movement, duration of the collar hold, etc.

- The grabber! In an emergency scenario you may be wanting someone else to grab Chad for you. If that's the case, recruit some friends and family to do a few repetitions for you.

Once we've done plenty of all of the above, we're going to add another important element: The lead...

Chad has learned to stay away from you in certain locations because being put on the lead has predicted the end of the fun. We're gonna flip that baby on its head. I want Chad to *know* that being put on the lead makes good things *happen*, not end...

1. Still in the living room by the settee where you've previously primed all of this good 'collar-grab' news, I want you to say 'Grab' and, as Chad leans his collar into your hand, hold his collar, clip the lead onto his harness, say 'Good!' and then MAKE IT LIKE A PARTY! Lots of individual treats, praise, cuddles, pictures of cats, etc... whatever Chad adores, pair it with the ceremony of the lead being clipped onto the harness.

2. Repeat the above several times but vary the latency, meaning the time between being put on the lead and the treats appearing. Sometimes one second,

sometimes up to five seconds. That way, in the future, as soon as you put Chad on the lead, he'll automatically focus and maintain his attention on you for a period of time, perhaps as you make your way away from the attractive French Poodle he's been courting.

3. Once you've done all of the above, we can then take it outside and begin our process of going 'live'. Head on out into the garden where there's little distraction but importantly, start from a position that's going to give you both the best chance to be successful. Start with Chad *next* to you, say 'Grab', hold his collar, clip the lead to his harness, say 'Good' and reinforce.

4. Now let's try the complete repertoire; say 'Come!' (see recall training pages 45-51), jog back a couple of steps as you face Chad running towards you, say 'Grab' ... hold the collar, clip the lead to the harness and let the good times roll!

Now you're flying and the only element left to add the cherry to the cake is to introduce the above exercise into your normal walking locations. Be pragmatic enough that when you go to the park to practise, you first repeat the very earliest elements of collar-grab training (settee optional) to remind Chad of the process and to be sure that you have a super-strong foundation. If in any doubt at all, have a long line attached to Chad's harness so he can't scarper and be inappropriately reinforced by ignoring you on his way to impress Madame La Poodle.

Judging from your letter, Chad's certainly learned what area of the walk guarantees 'the lead predicts bad news' and that's at the end of your walk. To that end, you're going to do many, many collar grabs/lead-ons during your walks in as many different locations as possible and to *make sure you pay well when the lead is on*. In fact, you can recall Chad, 'collar grab', pop the lead on his harness, say 'Good', and then treat, treat, treat, treat, as you walk with him a few steps, then take the lead off, stop the treats, and continue your walk. Now, it's not just one location, but several locations on your walk where you're going to give Chad *the opportunity to be put on the lead, earn a few treats, toys or cuddles and then be let off to explore again*. Do the 'lead-on = treats' many times at the end of each walk, near the car park before putting the lead on him for the final time and returning to your vehicle.

One vital closing point: make sure you reinforce heavily for that final 'lead-on'. It needs to predict the start of the jackpot, not the end of the fun.

There you go, I really hope that helps you both enjoy your walks even more; if it does, my work is done! If it doesn't, what do you want for £12.99 rrp?!

DOWN

Hi Steve,

I really enjoy your YouTube videos but can't find one on how to teach my dog a 'Down'. Do me a favour and spill the beans, will ya?

Best,
Bruce

Hi Bruce,

Nice to see you, to see you ... etc.

'Down' is a valuable exercise to teach any dog, especially
if you just want to hang out in a café or pub for a period of
time and enable your dog to 'switch-off' and relax (See also
'Settle', pages 174–9), and also when it's time for nail trims,
grooming, ear cleaning and cuddles. When meeting people
that may not be as confident around dogs as I am, especially
when I'm with my German Shepherd or my 'scourge of the
Daily Mail' Staffie, being able to pop my dog in a down
helps to put the other person at ease. So, with that many
useful applications, it is a behaviour that we really need to
get the hang of.

Here are several techniques...

LURE FROM A SIT

1. Ask your dog to 'Sit', if need be use a treat to
    lure their head up to get the sit. Once your dog
    is sitting, slowly move the treat in a straight line
    from your dog's nose down towards the ground
    and hold it between their feet. Often, as the dog's
    head drops to follow the treat, their butt lifts from
    the floor, D'oh! The reason for the butt-lift (very
    popular in LA, I believe), is that the head has been
    lured down, but also forward which causes the dog

to stand. If you find this is happening, make sure you lower the treat between their front paws, even a little behind their feet to under their elbows if needs be, this will remedy the problem of your dog tipping forward.

2. As your dog's chest and elbows make contact with the ground and they assume the Down position, say 'Good', to mark the behaviour, and give them a treat. At this stage, I'd like you to reinforce with several individual treats as your dog maintains their down. By doing so, not only will you reinforce the behaviour of the down being performed, but you'll also be showing your dog that remaining in that position pays dividends. If your dog chooses to get up, cool – simply stop the treats when they do get out of the down and next time feed more rapidly when they're in the desired position, you miser!

3. Repeat several times in the same location so you can create a nice predictable habit, then continue as above but say the word 'Down' as your dog assumes the position. When they hit the ground say 'Good', and reinforce.

This is the point where I need to digress and wonder why, for some reason, owners traditionally say all their other dog training cues in a jolly ol' hockey-sticks manner, such as 'Heeee-al', 'Siit-TA'. Yet weirdly, the cue 'Down' is often growled, all miserable-like, **<u>DOWN!</u>** ☹. It happens too often to just be a coincidence, but hey, don't you be one of those odd-bods; remember, when using positive reinforcement, a cue is a window of opportunity – *only good news is coming.*

Now that you're reliably getting a down partnered with your verbal cue, it's time to fade out the food lure being presented *before* the behaviour, and replace it with a food reinforcer *after* the behaviour. With the same body language, but with no treat in your hand, lure your dog's head down ... as their elbows and chest touch the ground, say 'Good', and produce a treat from your treat pouch with the other hand to reinforce the behaviour. Again, feel free to feed several individual treats as your dog remains in the down.

Over time, fade out your hand cue, so in future just the verbal cue will suffice. To do this, keep your verbal cue consistent but reduce your hand signal by 10% each session. This is particularly valuable if you're seven-foot tall, the proud owner of a Chihuahua but a martyr to your lumbago!

Now start adding *Duration*. Once your dog goes into a Down, wait two seconds before you say 'Good', then reinforce. Then wait five seconds, 10 seconds and so on... Every now and then throw in a quick one-second repetition just to keep your dog on their toes (not literally, that's too difficult from a down).

Now, add *Distraction* and *Proof* the behaviour. Practise in lots of different locations: indoors, outdoors, busy, quiet. *Proofing* means that you're making the behaviour nice and strong, resilient and reliable, by maintaining the same cue and behaviour in a myriad of differing environments and set-ups. Cue the behaviour with you standing, sitting and – here's one for the aficionados – with your back to the dog. Good luck with that one!

You can add *Distance* into your 3-Ds in two ways: firstly, by having a friend hold the lead or have your dog behind a gate as you take a few steps back and ask for a down. Secondly, you can ask for your down as above and, once your dog is in the correct position, take a few steps away to increase your distance. You can then return with your dog remaining in position, mark with a 'Good' and reinforce.

N.B. If your dog can't do a down on the first cue, don't get into the habit of issuing multiple cues. That's sloppy training. We want the cue for down to be 'Down'. Not 'Down, down, down, down, down, down. Good Boy!' Instead go back to an achievable level where one cue will suffice. Consolidate and build up from there.

Remember, we get what we train. Once you start issuing several verbal cues for down, you'll only get louder and ☹er!

EVOLVING THE DOWN: LURE FROM A STAND

Sometimes, in real-life scenarios, you'll want your dog to do a down from a sit position and sometimes from a standing position. We need to train for both possibilities because they are actually quite different mechanically for the dog – in the same way that for you, getting up from the floor requires a different movement to rising from a chair. Therefore, when luring from a standing position, follow all the stages as above but rather than starting from a sit position, do it from a standing position. This is particularly useful if you'd later like to progress to an Emergency Down.

When luring from a stand into a down position, don't be afraid to reinforce the incremental steps towards the final desired position. For example, spend a few sessions marking (with a 'Good') and reinforcing (with a treat) as your dog lowers their head to the floor ... Then mark and reinforce the lowering of the elbows ... Then reinforce the lowering of the chest to the floor. Once consistent, add your verbal cue and work through your 3-Ds of Duration, Distance and Distraction.

'CAPTURING' THE BATHROOM DOWN

This one's cute. Whereas down from a stand suggests a method called 'Shaping' (which is the reinforcement of incremental steps towards a final, target behaviour), our 'Bathroom Down' technique focuses on a training method called 'Capturing'.

To capture your dog's down, I want you to tip all the cards in your favour and to manipulate the environment as much as possible so you're not wasting your life away waiting for your dog to drop anchor.

Go with me on this one, but I want you to grab a good book (may I recommend *Easy Peasy Puppy Squeezy*, a 'rip-roaring-riot of puppy training antics' – Barry Manilow, possibly), a super-comfy dog blanket and a Tupperware pot of treats. Then head into the bathroom with your dog...

1. Put the treats out of reach of your dog and settle down to read your book...

   Ignore your dog, they'll no doubt want to have a little sniff around – let them, they'll soon get bored. Wandering about on the limited space offered by the tiled bathroom floor (if your bathroom floor is carpeted you don't need a dog trainer, you need a psychiatrist, or at least an interior designer and a jet wash!), your dog will soon decide to settle and on spotting the comfy blanket, will normally let out a sigh and lie down on the blanket. As soon as they do settle, gently say 'Good' and give them a treat, ideally as they continue to lie on the blanket. If they do get up when you say 'Good', and before you give them the treat, don't worry, still reinforce, just remember for next time don't shout 'GOOD!' so excitedly from inside a closed bathroom!

2. Keep your sessions short (someone may need the toilet), but you'll soon notice that when you go in again to put the blanket down on the bathroom floor, your dog will lie on it straight away in anticipation of their reward.

Great, it's now time to add the cue...

1. Place the blanket on the floor, as your dog goes through the motions of lying on it say 'Down'; once your dog is down on the blanket say 'Good' and reinforce with the treats.

2. Now that you've added your 'Down' cue, you can change locations to practise in different environments. The blanket won't be essential anymore; however, you'll be able to take advantage of the conditioning you've done with it when you move on to teach your 'Settle' training (see pages 174–9).

One final word on 'Down': if you notice any of your down training is getting a little 'sticky' or not progressing as you wish, make sure your dog has no injuries that may be making the behaviour uncomfortable and also check the surface you're asking your dog to lie on is comfortable and not something too tricky, such as a bare wooden floor or frosty ground.

Join me next week for a 10,000-word essay on dog trainers getting their knickers in a twist because owners say 'Down', when they really mean 'Off'...

ROMMIE DOG AND REFLEX TO NAME

Hey Steve,

We've been through a bit of an emotional roller coaster with our 'Rommie' dog Hagi who we finally welcomed into our London home six months ago. We guess he's around six years of age and, considering his background and journey to get to his forever home with us, I'm very happy to report that I think he's doing exceptionally well!

Although he loves his walks with me, sometimes as we're strolling along the pavement he'll just stop! He doesn't seem stressed at all, he just seems to want to have a good look around to check out the scenery. I honestly don't mind stopping with him and moving on when he's ready, it's just recently when we were 'glued' to the pavement, a family with a pram came towards us and unfortunately all I could do was pull Hagi with all my strength to one side so the family could pass. Obviously, I'd like to avoid 'man-handling' him like this, so if can you give me some tips to combat his selective-deafness, I'd be grateful!

Beryl

Hello Beryl,

Thanks for your letter and good to hear that things are mostly going in the right direction for you and Hagi. For the sake of our readers, let me explain what a Rommie dog is ... essentially a dog rescued from Romania and brought over to the UK to be adopted. Sadly, Romania has a hideously high stray dog population and often the dogs are treated poorly throughout the process of capture, being placed in a pound and, after 14 days, killed. Some dogs slip the net, are taken on by rescue organisations and, via a transport network of pick-ups and drop-offs, end up in homes throughout the UK. Many of the dogs come from an impoverished background, so to land in the UK, live in an actual house and be introduced to the hustle and bustle of what we consider 'normal', can be very overwhelming and lead to major issues. To be fair, it sounds like Hagi is taking it all in his stride. Good for him!

I'm going to suggest you teach Hagi an exercise I call a 'Reflex to Name' as a method to get his attention on to you when required, but first I want you to consider some 'rule-outs' to make sure there's no underlying factor we need to remedy first in connection with his standing still on walks:

🐾 Health: Maybe you have already, but if not, I'd like you to get a full vet work-up done for Hagi to make sure his sight, hearing, joints, etc. are all tickety-boo

and on point. I remember many years ago working with an English Bull Terrier who on day one I swore was deaf, that was until a colleague of mine opened a packet of crisps – I'd never seen a dog do a 180-degree turn and run to the source of a sound so quickly! (Turns out he wasn't deaf, I just wasn't saying anything worth listening to!)

- Overwhelm: Although Hagi is doing well, we need to remember that to him, arriving in London from the streets of Romania is the equivalent of us waking up to a Mardi Gras on Jupiter. Or a weekday in Luton. Sometimes when we're in a new place, full of different sights, sounds, smells and textures, we just need to stop and to try and slow down the information overload. It's fantastic that you have empathy in trumps here, illustrated by the fact that you're happy to stop and wait until he's ready before you move on together. That element of choice and control is extremely valuable to Hagi and will give him faith that you will allow him to experience things at his own pace. The ability to make choices is one of the most powerful and empowering freedoms we – dogs and humans – can have. To combat overwhelm, perhaps stick to repeating familiar walks for a while, to taper the bombardment of novelty. When going to a new environment with Hagi, don't see it as a 'walk' as such, see it as an opportunity to slow everything down, sit on a bench or under a tree and just watch the world go by together. He'll still get the benefit of the new exposure, but it'll be the difference between watching a Formula One Grand Prix from the stadium, as opposed to standing on the track itself!

Variables: Get your detective hat on. Is there any common denominator that you can detect on the days he does stop?

- Time of day?

- Darkness?

- Different handler?

- Weather?

If you do find a particular sticky point that causes Hagi to put the brakes on, gently expose him to that specific element in a non-pressurised way to gradually build up his confidence and to help him become more comfortable in that environment.

Finally, before explaining reflex to name, I want to make sure you haven't been *inadvertently* reinforcing the behaviour. I've had a few similar cases where the dog has been stopping on walks. During the initial consultation and assessment, I've asked the owner one of my go-to questions – 'What do YOU do when he stops?' On more than one occasion, the reply has been, 'Well, we pull out a treat to encourage him to start walking again...'

Q: How does the dog train the monkey to produce food?

A: Stop!

We always get what we train. Dog – 1; Human – 0

REFLEX TO NAME

So, with the above ruled out, let's look at teaching the reflex to name. To get Hagi to give you attention, a reflex to name will act like the power-steering you desire without the need for physical force. It's a slightly unusual method of initially training a behaviour, because whether Hagi gets the treat or not, *is not contingent on whether he looks to you or not*. I know, anarchy, right. (Like red wine with fish.)

We're not initially pairing the treat with the behaviour, but rather pairing the treat with the sound of his name:

1. Sit in a nice quiet, familiar location with Hagi.

2. Have a decent supply of treats in your treat pouch, but *not* in your hand. I don't want the predictor to be *treat in hand*, I want the *sound of his name* being the predictor of the good news.

3. After a few moments of quiet, simply say 'Hagi!' *then* place your hand in the treat pouch, pull out a treat and give it to him. Importantly, Hagi's behaviour here is sort of irrelevant, whether he looks to you or not isn't important. The value lies in the fact that when you say 'Hagi', he gets a treat. That's the deal.

4. Count a few seconds then repeat ... and again, and again.

5. Sometimes wait five seconds between repetitions. Sometimes wait 20 seconds, sometimes two minutes. You'll soon build a nice strong association between the sound of his name and the delivery of the treats. Try and be as consistent as possible with your tone and volume, and you'll soon see the penny drop for Hagi, as the second he hears his name ... BOOM, he won't be able to stop himself from turning towards you – like a reflex.

It's vital that you do the initial stage of this training in a very quiet area to build the foundations of your power-steering. When you're hitting 20 out of 20 with Hagi snapping his head around to look at you when you say his name, increase the distraction, hit 20 out of 20, then upgrade the environment again.

If you call his name and he doesn't check-in, no biggie,

it's just too soon. You already appreciate the value of going at Hagi's pace, so simply go back a step or two to a less distracting environment to consolidate, and build from there. **Training is a process, not an event.**

Because of your specific request, make sure you do lots of sessions with Hagi on the lead; it's important we practise for what we'll eventually want out in the real world. To practise for the incoming-pram scenario – or worse still, freezing in the middle of the road – say 'Hagi' then take a few steps back so he gets used to *following* you to claim his prize. That should suffice to create the necessary elbow room on the pavement or to escape the on-coming traffic!

If you live in a super-vocal household with 'Hagi-this' and 'Hagi-that' being shouted all the time with no real consequence, do the above exercise but rather than using his name, come up with your own irresistible special word or sound. What makes it irresistible isn't the sound of the word, but what it *means* to Hagi. With my multi-dog households, I use the word 'Yip'!

Teaching Hagi the reflex to name exercise will certainly help you to get his attention, but bear in mind, **it's always worth prioritising how he *feels* over what he *does*,** so in all aspects of his new life with you, continue to go at his pace and give him every opportunity to make his own right choices.

It sounds like you've both won the lottery, enjoy your lives together, he's a lucky boy!

EMERGENCY STOP

Hi Steve,

My Toy Poodle Magnus and I enjoy long walks in the countryside. He's very good off-lead, but, as we go from field to field, for my own peace of mind I like to keep Magnus in sight. I wondered if it's possible for me to teach him to stop when he's ahead of me, rather than me having to pop him on a lead or recall him every time we're about to go around a corner?

In addition, when he was younger, he once squeezed past me at the front door and ran to the other side of the road. Calling him would have been dangerous, so again, some kind of emergency stop would be wonderful!

Mrs. A.E. Warburton

Hi Mrs Warburton,

I've got the perfect exercise for you and Magnus! *Emergency Stop!*

    This is a real show-boating exercise to teach your dog! If you're in a safe, secure area, feel free to do this with Magnus off the lead. If you have any doubts, have a loose five-metre long line attached to your dog's harness.
Let's do it!

EMERGENCY STOP

1. Drop three or four treats on the floor for your dog to enjoy; the reason you're doing this is to buy you some time to sneak away from him.

2. As he's grazing, take a few steps backwards away from him, five or six is fine, just enough to give you a bit of distance from each other.

3. Have one treat in your hand and *as soon as Magnus finishes the treats from the ground and looks up to you,* raise your treat-holding hand above your head like a traffic policeman and say 'STOP!', count a beat in your head then on the second beat throw the treat over Magnus's head so it lands just behind his butt. Note: how you deliver the treat is *very* important.

When you say, 'STOP!', I need you to have a nice clear hand signal. There'll be times in the future when your dog will be a distance away from you, so the additional insurance of a visual cue will be a real bonus. Also, bear in mind that a verbal cue will sound very different five metres away than it will when you're 50 metres away. An arm over your head will always just be an arm over your head!

The reason I want your arm raised in the air *above* your head is because that will show a clear silhouette for your dog to pick up on; if your arm is just put out in front of you, then the signal will be lost in the rest of your body's outline.

The movement of your arm should come in two parts, like a dart player throwing a dart. You know the way they do a little fake throw first, then on the second repetition they throw it? That's what I want you to do, but I want you to say 'STOP!' on the first repetition, then throw the treat on the second repetition. The reason we have the 'two beats' process is that we want to condition that the first one – when you say 'STOP!' – predicts that the treat is coming on the second repetition.

'STOP!' *followed* by treat.
Not STOP *and* treat at the same time.

It's also very important that the treat lands behind your dog's butt. We ultimately want your dog to freeze on the spot in anticipation when you say 'Stop'. If the treat is delivered *in front* of the dog, then we're inadvertently going to be rewarding him for creeping forward. No good at throwing? No problem. Practise. Get better!

With enough repetition, the dog sees your arm in the air, you do the first traffic cop movement and say 'Stop!' ... What does the dog do in anticipation of the treat landing behind their butt? That's right, they STOP! We're in business.

Now that the conditioning has taken place, you can decide your own next step. Perhaps throw the treat behind their butt to reinforce as before. Perhaps you walk over to your stationary dog and treat them in situ. Perhaps throw a toy for your dog to chase. Or perhaps reinforce by simply saying 'Off you go!', and allowing your dog to go off and enjoy their walk.

Here's the bit that gets some people's knickers in a twist... So often owners are told to only treat once the behaviour has been done correctly –well, not so for this gig. Why? You need to ask yourself the question: '*What does it mean to the dog?*'

I'll often ask owners, 'When you say "Stop!", what does it mean to your dog?' They'll answer, 'To stand still'. Then they'll notice me raise an eyebrow. They'll offer, 'To not move forward?' My other brow elevates. With this training protocol, when we say 'STOP!', it simply means to the dog '*a treat is going to land behind my butt*'. That's it.

And we're true to our word. Every time we say 'STOP!' in training, a treat *does* land behind the dog's butt. In the early stages, we don't even need to focus on whether the dog is moving or not when we say 'Stop'. We're just rock-solid-hang-your-hat-on-consistent every time: 'STOP!' means a treat *will* land behind the dog's butt. Initially, we're *conditioning the word*, not *reinforcing the behaviour*.

Now, once we've done a good few repetitions and the penny's dropped for the dog about what 'STOP!' actually means, then as a *by-product* the dog will drop anchor when the cue's given. NOW we can start to reinforce the desired behaviour.

Once you're saying 'STOP!' and your dog immediately stands still, you can start adding more distance between the two of you before giving the cue, start practising in different locations and maybe start to add a bit of duration between your dog stopping and you delivering the reward.

Tips:

- 🐾 Use treats that are large enough and contrast in colour sufficiently to stand out on the surface you're training on.

- 🐾 Feel free to use a long line but avoid any tension.

- 🐾 This is a skill, practise it. Go into your garden and practise throwing 10 individual treats into a plant pot. Each time you score eight or more, yay! Take two steps further back and go again. If you score less than seven, go two steps closer, you big

loser! You will definitely not look mad in front of your neighbours. (But do it in the back garden, not the front!)

The emergency stop is a super-important behaviour to teach your dog, not only for maximum control and safety but just as importantly, if anyone's watching it looks really, *really* cool!

PART 2
PROBLEM BEHAVIOURS AND HOW TO HELP

Like all of us, dogs do the behaviours that they think are right for them to do at any given time.

Dogs do the behaviours that *work*.

A lot of the time these *problem* behaviours come out because the dog is stressed, scared or simply doesn't know what else to do in such circumstances to get what they need. Our approach in the following pages is two-fold: firstly, we'll address the underlying emotional fuel behind the fire that is triggering the problem behaviour. Secondly, we'll teach the dog a more appropriate, mutually exclusive and acceptable behaviour that will give them, and us, the outcomes we're searching for.

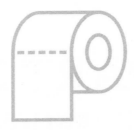

COPROPHAGIA

Steve,

Help!

My young Labrador Sally eats her own poop in the garden and I have no idea why! I've started to rush to pick it up as soon as she goes to the toilet but I suspect she's now racing to beat me to it. What can I do, she's driving me nuts (and making me feel sick!)?

Gemma

Hi Gemma,

Okay, we'll come up with a solution for you shortly, but first to your question of 'Why?' To be fair to Sally – and from her perspective – '*why not?*'

I'm not saying, 'Don't knock it till you try it', but to an animal whose ancestors had to potentially spend huge amounts of energy to get their nutrients, as well as run the risk of injury and conflict just to get a square meal, it makes sense to eat it off her own doorstep and, if she's quick enough, it's still warm! Sorry.

Suffice as to say, even though the food has been eaten, then digested, then ... let's keep it civil , shall we ... 'passed', there's still nutrients there to be had. Still some 'meat on the bone', so to speak. It's disgusting, isn't it?

Maybe if we called it by its exotic name it might take the edge off things: *coprophagia* – from the Greek *copros*, meaning 'faeces' and *phagein*, meaning 'to eat'.

No, doesn't improve matters, does it? Like when they tried to change the name of Barnet in north London to Barnét. We all still knew.

So, one of the reasons Sally may be eating poop is because of the 'cheap' access to nutrients. First up, ensure Sally's diet is of a premium quality and that she has no digestion issues. Another potential motivator may be found if we wind the clock back to Sally's puppyhood. For the first few weeks of a litter's life, it's the mother's duty to get rid of any waste left by the pups by eating the poop; she does this to keep the area clean, and maybe even to prevent the smell from attracting predators. So, there may be a bit of 'monkey see, monkey do' going on here.

I recall once doing a home visit and sadly the owner had inadvertently encouraged the *coprophagia* by telling his dog off for toileting inside. Acting upon poor advice, the owner had rubbed his dog's nose in the poop when he was shocked to find the mess on his carpet. Rather than exploring *why* the dog had felt the need to go to the toilet inside (Stress? Lack of outdoor opportunity? Illness? Poor toilet training?), the owner had just focused on *what* the dog had done, and tried to deliver the punishment to fit the crime. Poor dog.

The dog's stress and lack of toilet training continued, which meant that he still had to go to the toilet inside; however, as the dog had been *taught* that 'bad things happen if the owner sees the poop on the carpet', the dog had learned to swallow the evidence. Thankfully, after unwinding the issues, building the dog's trust, heavily reinforcing for toileting outside and flushing the owner's head down the toilet (kidding!), it all came good. But that entire situation could so easily have been avoided.

So, on to what you can proactively do; how can you break the habit?

For a start, make sure there is no dog waste in your

Body Language

Square, straight & staring:
Bad news

Soft spine & bends in the body:
Good news!

The contagious yawn. Try it!

Loose Lead Walking

Dog on the right...

...dog on the left

Happiness is when the dog, the lead and the monkey are all smiling!

Chin Rest

Teaching The Down

"She said 'Yes!'" 💍

Emergency Stop

No good at throwing?
Practice!

Teaching a gentler take

Play is training for real life

Eye Contact and Focus

Leg Weaves

Peek-A-Boo: Feet-On

"So embarrassing Dad!"

Luring the Spin

Bow

garden. If you need to do a 'picking-up session', then go ahead, open a bottle of wine, invite a few friends round, it'll be fun! Importantly though, *do it out of the sight* of Sally. We don't want her thinking that YOU love it too!

At the moment Sally is in the habit of pooping, then immediately turning around and eating it. Let's create a new habit. While we're training, I need you to consistently go out into the garden with Sally at toileting time. The very split-second she poops, I want you to enthusiastically call her to you and shower her with treats for a fantastic recall (see pages 45–51).

I need *this* to be the new habit formed in Sally's mind:

a) I poop

b) Gemma calls me

c) I run to Gemma and get the best treats!

To create this habit, you need to be consistent, accurate and generous. Stay consistent with your recalls and make sure you call her to run to you, as opposed to you running to her. Don't make it a 'race to the bottom'!

After several sessions of you calling Sally as soon <u>as she poops</u>, she'll quickly start to put Number Two and two together and she'll learn to cut out the 'middle-man'. There'll be no need for you to verbally do your recall anymore, as the association, and therefore the new behaviour, will have been formed. You will have shifted the old habit into a far healthier and more attractive one. Go you!

JUMPING UP

Hi Steve,

We need your expertise!

Our Irish Setter Ruby is a real sweetheart but we recently had to have a dog trainer visit us at home to help us stop her from jumping up at visitors when they come through the front door. The trainer was very nice and explained that we had inadvertently been rewarding Ruby for jumping up by allowing visitors to give her cuddles and attention when she did so. That made perfect sense, so for the last fortnight we've asked visitors to ignore her when they come in ... but the jumping up has gotten worse! On some occasions, it's been so unbearable and frustrating that the only way we've been able to calm her down has been to let the visitors say 'Hello' to her just to make the jumping stop.

Now what?!

Mark

Hi Mark,

So close, but yet...!

Your trainer is right in saying that to stop a behaviour, we also need to stop the reinforcement; however, that's just one-third of the remedy required.

The three-pronged solution I'd offer is this:

1. Make sure the unwanted behaviour doesn't get reinforced.

2. Reinforce our Active Ingredient Two – a Mutually Exclusive Behaviour (MEB): this sounds fancy but remember, it is simply a behaviour that, if the dog is doing the MEB, then they can't physically do the unwanted behaviour at the same time. In this case, a great MEB would be a sit. Ruby can't sit and jump up at the same time.

   The trick here is to heavily reinforce Ruby when she sits, especially in the hallway and near the front door. She needs to learn that, 'All good things come to those that sit.'

   The excitement and history of (inadvertent) reinforcement at the front door may well be too high a criterion to start with, so for the next few days practise her sit in the garden, the living room, out on walks. Work through the 3-Ds of

Distraction, Duration and Distance to make her sit nice and solid, then start edging the training set-up nearer and nearer to the desired finished product of asking Ruby to sit when someone comes through the front door. Practise with several 'stooge' visitors, starting with passive arrivals, and progress through to more exciting and animated guests. When you're at that point, make sure she's showered with the *über*-reinforcement of not only treats, but also the attention and cuddles she obviously loves. You know what she wants, the training is just a way of showing her how to get it so all parties are happy. If you have a doorbell or door knocker, make sure that you throw that sound into your practice sessions also, so you can really proof your training for when you go 'live'.

3. Control and Management
   Our Active Ingredient Four, C&M, is a very important tool to have in our dog training locker. It may not be the most rock 'n' roll feature in the package, but it's there to ensure that point (one) above, doesn't rear its ugly head to put us back at the starting line.
   Continue to work through your sit training in many different locations and scenarios, with a view to Ruby being able to sit by the front door for a

visitor when asked to do so. However, *until* she can sit in the presence of an exciting visitor, don't put her in the position to make a mistake, and to be inadvertently reinforced for jumping up all over again. Until Ruby's ready, if the doorbell goes unexpectedly and you've not got your dog training hat on, pop her in the garden or another room *before* you open the front door. That way jumping up can't be reinforced, frustration will be avoided and your training will stay on track.

Warning: some dog trainers that opt for aversive punishments for jumping up may well pipe in with, 'You're just avoiding the problem'. If they do, simply stroke their hair and tell them you love them. They love that.

Another behavioural spanner in the works you're experiencing is what's called an *Extinction Burst*. When a behaviour, in this case jumping up, gets reinforced, in this case with cuddles, then that behaviour is more likely to occur again in the future. Your trainer was right to advise that to stop the behaviour, you need to stop the reinforcement, however ... when a behaviour has a long history of being reinforced, it means even though the reinforcement has suddenly ceased, the behaviour may actually increase for a while as a kind of last ditch death-roll to try and make the reinforcement kick in to play again. Let me tell you a story...

Many moons ago I used to write for several dog magazines. I still write for some even though I'd rather be out with my dogs than stuck in a room writing, gazing out of the window like a werewolf-Charlie Brown. A friend of mine, Andy, who has his own offices, said, 'Look, you big baby. Why don't you use my spare office to write without the distraction of dogs, and then when you're done you can go off and do whatever the hell it is that you do!'

So that's what we'd do, meet in the car park and make our way to Andy's offices, which were in a kind of a management suite with a shared reception area. Now, every day, without fail, Andy would head over to the vending machine, insert 50p (that's how long ago it was!) press A-4, out would come a Mars Bar™, then up to the studio we would go...

Next day, 50p ... A-4 ... Mars Bar
Next day, 50p ... A-4 ... Mars Bar
Next day, same...
Day after, same...

Then one day we met up as normal, Andy went 50p ... A-4 ... nothing. NOTHING!

Andy's. World. Was. Rocked! He pressed A-4 again ... nothing ... then he pressed A-4 harder, **angrier**.........**A! 4! A! 4!** No matter how hard he now thumped the buttons, nothing, no Mars Bar. Livid!

What you've witnessed there is Andy's behaviour going

through an 'Extinction Burst'. We know that when a behaviour occurs and it gets reinforced, it's more likely to happen again in the future. The more you do that behaviour and it gets reinforced each time, the deeper ingrained it becomes. So, when it *doesn't* get reinforced one day, you will still try that behaviour again (and often harder, faster, louder, more intensely), because you think, '*It ALWAYS gets reinforced, what's wrong?!*'

If the behaviour *still* doesn't get reinforced, THEN it becomes extinct. THEN you'll stop offering the behaviour. The effort/benefit ratio will have been knocked out of kilter and you'll walk away.

That's behaviour, that's evolution. That's Mars Bars.

That's why Ruby's jumping up has become *more* intense since the reinforcement has been switched off. The good news is you don't have to surf through the frustration of an extinction burst because of the watertight C&M and MEB that you are going to introduce which will take care of that potential banana skin for you.

Now, back to Andy ... Let's say the vending machine actually wanted to increase the intensity of Andy's behaviour in exchange for a Mars Bar. It would've built up a history of reinforcement (50p + A-4 = Mars Bar), similar to you building up a history of reinforcement for Ruby when she's jumped up at visitors in the past (jumping up = cuddles). However, after a while the machine doesn't drop a Mars Bar for A-4. It waits until Andy increases the intensity: A-4

... A-4 ... AA-44 ... Boom! When Andy thumps AA-44, the Mars Bar drops. The machine has now set a new standard. Andy has 'learned' that the way to get what he wants is to offer the new, more intense version of behaviour. Again, Ruby's jumping up has mirrored this sequence.

Jumping up = Cuddles
(Trainer advises) Jumping up = Zero
(Extinction Burst) 'Unbearable' INTENSE jumping up = Cuddles!

Don't worry, you've not created a monster. C&M again saves the day!

This is your chance to apply three of our Active Ingredients as a 'holy trinity' to solve the puzzle:

1. *Don't* reinforce the unwanted behaviour of jumping up
2. *Do* reinforce the MEB of sit
3. Ensure the C&M is watertight until the training kicks in.

In a way, your problem is a lovely one to have: you live with a dog that adores people ... the amount of clients I've worked with that would give their right arm for such a problem!

Get your training back on track and soon Ruby will be able to politely spread the love once again.

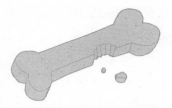

TREAT GRABBING

Hi Steve,

We've an adorable seven-month-old Malinois named Jessie who absolutely loves to learn and excitedly does a little 'dance' when she knows we're about to do some training. However, she actually gets herself into a bit of a frenzy, such that I'm sure most of the lesson doesn't actually sink in. The main problem we're having is biting our hands when we're trying to give her treats. The hand-nipping is particularly bad at our training classes as she gets so 'high' when we're in the main hub of other dogs, it's like she can't control herself. We've tried telling her 'Wait' and 'Gently' but then she just seems to explode onto the food when we do finally give her the release. We've also tried to withdraw the treat if it looks like she's going to snatch, but to no avail. She desperately wants the food, so I'm guessing she's not too aroused or anxious? It's just that she's so excited and frantic that her teeth coincidently pinch ... and hurt!

Jenny

Hi Jenny,

I've been lucky enough to train hundreds of Malinois and I've lived with two in the past: ASBO, my first Mali, and Carlos, my most recent one who I talk about in *Easy Peasy Puppy Squeezy*. Each were amazing dogs and each were, like Jessie, *Maligators* when it came to taking treats. Believe me, I've felt your pain!

The good news is, I've made all the mistakes and taken a few hits for the team so you don't have to. Take some advice from an old fool and follow my list of Dos & Don'ts to save your sanity, and your fingers...

AROUSAL

Arousal: not always necessarily good, not always necessarily bad, but certainly a contributing factor when looking at *urgent behaviour* as described.

Depending on the specific behaviour, added arousal will make that behaviour faster, louder, harder, more intense. Look at the intensity of the jockey patting his horse in congratulations after a neck-and-neck photo finish of a high stakes race. Because arousal is so high, the jockey slaps the horse's neck with force that would make the horse bolt if he did that before the race. How about the unusually tight grip the little girl has on her teddy bear as she nears the front of the queue to greet Santa or the white knuckles gripping the front of the roller coaster carriage before it's even moved.

First things first, we need to make sure Jessie isn't being asked to *learn* in an environment that is too arousing for her to be able to cope and absorb the lesson being presented. **Dogs are always learning *something*; we just need to make sure they're learning what we hope we're teaching**.

If you continually put Jessie next to dogs in class and she repeatedly gets aroused, the lesson learned by her may well be, *When I'm near dogs, I get over-aroused*.

Fast-forward to tomorrow and she sees another dog at the park, how have we taught her to behave?

If you're going to continue to go to your local dog classes, I want you to contact your dog trainer first and arrange how you can change the environment set-up so Jessie doesn't feel so aroused. A phrase I often use with my owners sounds obvious but it is a core truth in dog training, 'To change something, we need to change something.'

To change behaviour, we often need to first change the environment. I don't want you to keep going back into the same environment and just hoping for a change in behaviour.

Potential changes that can made to the group class training environment for you and Jessie are:

Distance

Distance is always our friend when working with over-arousal. Increase the distance you and Jessie are working away from the main 'hub' of the class. As the weeks pass, and as long as Jessie stays below her arousal threshold, gradually decrease the distance you're working away from the hub. This process is called desensitisation and will prove very effective, as long as you don't try to run before you can walk.

Arrival/Exit

Can you arrange to arrive early to class? We really don't want Jessie to be steaming into class with the excitement of all of the other dogs rolling in also, like the doors of a Metallica concert being flung open for everyone to rush down to the front of the stage. Ideally, have Jessie arrive 10 minutes earlier, let her have a sniff around to ground herself, then settle into your space together, sit on the floor and give her a massage. Associate relaxation with the environment, not over-excitement. Leave early or leave late, whichever offers the most mellow exit.

Barriers

Can physical barriers be used to cut down the visual stimulation of the class activities? Herding breeds can very easily get turned on by movement. They can also potentially get very frustrated if not permitted to 'control' others' movement within their environment.

Class Culture

We don't try and start to teach Maths to kids on a roller coaster. Are the class culture and the exercises being offered conducive to Jessie staying below threshold? Contrary to popular belief, group classes shouldn't be frenzied piranha tanks of owners desperately trying to be 'the most fun thing in the hall', but rather an environment of controlled connection between dog and owner.

Getting back to snatching treats out of your hand, you mention that she's 'not too aroused or anxious as she still wants the food'; however, the deal isn't as simple as 'over-aroused = can't take food'. Over-arousal or anxiety won't necessarily stop a dog from taking food, but it will certainly contribute to a more frenzied urgency in the grabbing of the food. Here are some ideas to work with...

THE DON'TS

Waiting

Telling a dog to 'wait' for treats or food is like being stuck at an amber traffic light for far too long. You're poised, waiting ... waiting ... come on! When is it *finally* going to go green? ... then ... BOOM! The light goes green. You will ALWAYS drive off faster from a painfully long amber light because you've been asked to compress and supress the behaviour that you actually want to do. That's why

Jessie sometimes waits, waits, waits, *then* 'explodes' onto the food.

Ego Depletion

This is another spanner in the works when we're trying to rely on impulse control to limit treat snatching. Ego depletion illustrates how impulse control and willpower draw from a limited well of resources that can eventually run out.

What on earth is ego depletion, I hear you say? Well, have you ever been sat at home *knowing* that there's a lovely full packet of biscuits in the cupboard but NO, you're on a diet, you're going to be good.

No biscuits for me, you say to yourself at 7pm ... and at 8pm ... and at 9.

Not one, you say at 9.15pm. *Not even ½ a biscuit*, you say at 9.17pm as you try to distract yourself with a thin, paltry, jilted cup of tea.

You've called upon all of your reserves of impulse control and by 10pm you're ever so proud of yourself ... but by 10.01pm YOU'VE EATEN THE WHOLE PACKET OF BISCUITS and are desperately looking in the boot of the car for a second pack!

You've asked too much of yourself, you've drained the willpower battery far too much and if only you'd had one biscuit at 7pm when you first fancied one, you would've had every chance of avoiding the McVitie's tsunami that was inevitably to follow.

To that end, I want you to look at *all* of Jessie's training holistically, with an emphasis on wafer-thin increases to the *duration* element of each exercise.

For example, when you are out on her walk, add a second at a time to the duration between her sitting at the curb, and you reinforcing the sit by saying 'good' and continuing her walk.

Another example would be adding a second at a time to you opening the boot of your car and you then saying 'Good', and releasing her from the vehicle to play with you in the park. Or adding a second at a time to you having your hand on the back-door handle, Jessie giving you eye contact and you saying 'Good' before opening the door for her to go outside and explore. It's these little delays in the gratification that will help her keep calm and not become desperate to reach her goal at 100mph every time. All good things come to those that wait.

Withdrawing Food

When trying to resolve grabbing and snatching, another method that sometimes delivers undesired results is the technique of withdrawing the food if she's going to snatch at it. In my book, this can easily add frustration and desperation – two ingredients we really don't want to add into the mix if we can help it!

Ever play the game 'Hungry Hippos'? The name of the game is for each player to operate their hippo to grab at the marbles. Watch people playing: the more they miss, the harder and faster they try to operate their hippo next time around. Whack-a-Mole is another example, the more you miss, the harder you hit next time.

As well as increasing frustration, withdrawing a treat the dog thought they were going to get will also build disappointment, suspicion and conflict, none of those are welcome in *Easy Peasy Doggy Squeezy*!

Okay, so it's all well and good me telling you what *not to do* but that's not so constructive is it? Let me to tell you what you *can* actually do to help improve the treat-taking situation.

Taking treats gently is a *concept* rather than a cued behaviour, so there's no need to add a verbal cue of 'Gently' or 'Take it'; changing the arousal levels, offering the food in a different manner and choosing our battles will be enough to get us, and keep us, on the right track.

THE DOS

Body Language

If you see Jessie is getting too revved-up in training, don't keep ploughing away and expect a change. Simply stop the training and do what you can to help Jessie 'come down' and relax; change or leave the environment, slow down, massage, ear rub – whatever it takes. **Remember: To change something ... change something.**

You'll know she's getting too revved-up by noticing that her movements and whole cadence become faster, more staccato. Her ears and tail may become more erect, her mouth may change from being open and relaxed to closed and tight. Perhaps her pupils have become dilated ... take benchmark readings of Jessie's body language when she's relaxed, so you can note and react when she's becoming over-aroused.

Treat Delivery

I want you to practise your treat delivery to Little Miss Snipermouth *away* from any arousing group class environment and independently away from any other exercise such as sit or down.

Start with boring, low-value 'nothing-to-write-home-about' treats such as cubes of carrot or apple and, for all of the exercises listed on the following pages, gradually work through the 'food-value-grades' as Jessie continues to use a soft mouth to take the treats. Don't improve the menu choices until a consistent soft mouth is offered.

All of the training will initially commence when you're at home, probably of an evening when you're both chilled out and ideally as Jessie is crashed out, half comatose on the floor and 'floppy'. Use large, easy to 'mouth target' treats and a product that's non-crumbly to avoid a sudden gold rush!

1. With Jessie lying down and you sat on the floor next to her, place the treat between your middle two fingers, close your fist and offer the treat to Jessie's mouth with the treat poking out of the back of your fist. The only way Jessie will be able to take the treat, and therefore the method she'll practise and be reinforced for adopting, will be to gently use her tongue, not her teeth.

   NB: It's important here that you notice I tell you to *offer the treat to Jessie's mouth*. Practise delivering the treat *to* Jessie, which will in turn break the habit of Jessie feeling the need to lunge and grab *at* the treat. Too many people dangle the food for the dog to grab at and, of course, this is what we want to avoid.

   If you spend your childhood only eating at sushi bars where the culture is to grab at food from the conveyor belt as it rotates, you're going to be a nightmare in posh restaurants as you continue to snatch food destined for other diners from the passing waiter's silver tray!

2. Progress to offering the treat to Jessie's mouth from an open hand, palm up, with your thumb covering the treat between the base of your middle two fingers. As you feel Jessie's tongue work the treat, release it for her.

3. From the thumb-over-treat method, evolve to offer the treat to Jessie's mouth from a simple open hand, like you're feeding a horse. Again, there's no benefit, and therefore no need for Jessie to use her teeth. It's a gentle mouth and use of the tongue that gets reinforced.

If at any stage Jessie uses her teeth to grab at the treat, go back a step or two, ensure the next session is delivered in a very relaxed and 'lazy' set-up, ensure the treats are low value and ensure you're delivering to the mouth, rendering grabbing redundant.

When you can comfortably give Jessie treats in a down, graduate onto working through all four stages with her in a sit, then with the pair of you on the move as you slowly walk together off-lead at first, then on-lead so you can practise your lead-handling and treat-delivery skills together.

Food or Toys?

Sometimes when fingers are continually being nipped as the dog grabs at the treats, owners are tempted to move from food to toys as a reinforcer. Toys and, more importantly, play are fantastic weapons to have in your arsenal of potential reinforcers; however, if the dog is already over-aroused, then adding an anticipation to 'Chase, Grab and Bite' are not the best activities to throw into an already high-octane mix. The sensible route is to lower arousal and use food correctly, as opposed to associating more adrenalin with the training exercises and then wondering why the dog's eyes start spinning the next time we say 'Sit'.

Don't get me wrong, I adore using play, not only as a reinforcer but just for the sheer joy of it; however, for an already 'high' grabby dog it can give the false impression of a quick fix. I want to adopt a 'root and branch' approach here, not just a 'let's just try and survive the day' mentality.

To avoid sounding like the Fun Police, I want you to know that I use tons of toy play in my training, but I like to use it at the right time. When I'm teaching a new behaviour to a dog, I will definitely opt for food over toys first because:

- I can do a lot more repetitions over a shorter duration with food than I can with toys.

  The more successful repetitions I can do, the quicker the lesson becomes ingrained.

- Once I give a treat, the dog is instantly ready and asking to do the behaviour again. Hurrah!

- Once I give a toy, before I can ask for a repetition of the behaviour again, I need to take the toy away from the dog. Boo!

🐾 The dog's mental stamina is longer, therefore permitting more quality repetitions when using food rather than a quicker burnout rate and losing focus when using high-energy play.

So, you ask, when DO you use toys and play as reinforcers?

Once I've done many repetitions – and I'm talking hundreds – of a particular behaviour and reinforced with food to the standard I'm aiming at, *if* I then want to add more speed, urgency or intensity to the behaviour, *then* I'll introduce toys to give me that extra turbo boost.

Some behaviours, such as recall or emergency downs, are ones that I'll always aim at improving the speed, so those bad boys will definitely have toys and play introduced at some stage. By contrast, some exercises, such as settle or nail trimming protocols (see pages 174 and 180), are ones that I'll always want to be associated with relaxation and 'rest and digest', so chances are I'll stick with food for those.

As a tip, if you ever want to add more speed to an exercise but still want to use food, then try rolling the food along the floor for the dog to chase and grab. That's a sure-fire way to ignite the predator within!

I'm reminded of a home visit I did many years ago for a Jack Russell that the family had nicknamed 'Oven Glove' because it was the essential bit of kit needed for anyone in the household that was going to attempt to give him a treat!

I'm sure Jessie's not so bad; the important consideration is to look at the bigger picture first. Make sure the environment is conducive to being relaxed, read her body language to measure arousal levels and slowly work through the treat-placement protocols as described.

Jessie sounds so much like many of the dogs I've had the joy to share my life with in the past. It's that *carpe diem* enthusiasm for life that makes them so wonderful to be around, but by teaching her to slow down and relax, she'll be able to enjoy life *and* smell the *roses at the same time.

*fox poo, dogs' butts, visitors' groins ...

REACTIVITY

Hi Steve,

I live with Polly, my little Jack Russell, and I've been getting some conflicting advice about helping with her reactivity to other dogs. She's really not great at coping with bigger dogs and even if they're friendly, should they get too close then she'll bark and lunge at them until they back off. On some occasions, the other dog (or owner!) hasn't got the message, so I've resorted to having to pick her up to make our escape. Here lies the bone of contention: some people have told me I should never pick her up as that will make her worse. My trainer says I wouldn't pick her up if she were a German Shepherd, so I should deal with her 'as if she were a normal dog' and treat her with a firm hand. I know her aggression is probably my fault, I just don't want to make her any worse and I'd love your advice as to how to help.

Best,
Margaret

Hi Margaret,

Change your trainer. '... As if she were a *normal* dog'! I promise you, Polly *is* a normal dog.

As a little dog, from Polly's perspective, being afraid of GIANT dogs is perfectly normal. I'd love to see your trainer act 'as if they were a normal human' should they be approached by a bouncy, grinning 20-foot-tall human, while the giant's owner shouted from 100 metres away, 'It's okay, he's friendly!'

A lot of my early career working with dogs was in the security sector, so I'm well used to hearing the 'dogs need a firm hand' gubbins. No dog needs a 'firm hand'. What they *do* need is:

🐾 Clear instructions and reinforcement so they make more right choices

🐾 Control and Management so they don't make bad choices.

🐾 Protection from scary things.

It's not a big ask, is it?

Also, don't you go blaming yourself by saying Polly's behaviour is 'your fault'. I don't buy into the 'There's no such thing as bad dogs, only bad owners' red herring. There are owners that care, and owners that don't. It's always the owners that care that have enough guilt to start their own religion. You're obviously one of the good guys or you wouldn't have cared enough to write this letter so, from now on, you relax, the pressure's on me.

I've lived with many dogs, mostly big 'uns such as German Shepherds and Malinois. However, more recently, the God-of-Failed-Foster-Dogs has deemed to bless me with a few little 'uns including Nancy, the love of my life Chihuahua x Terrier x Beelzebub, weighing in at an impressive sod-all, soaking wet. One of my guilty pleasures is making up names when people ask me what breed she is. So far, I've got away with a Chicago Hustler, a Snapperoo, a Fox Meddler and, my favourite to date, a High-Jinx Harrier! Living with Nancy has increased my empathy for smaller dogs because to look after her well, I need to consider the world *from her perspective*. She's living in the Land of Giants.

Polly sounds a lot like Nancy when I first took her on a few years ago, so I'm going to tell you some of the key points that we worked on together to make living in the Land of Giants a little less scary for her. Nancy was found abandoned running around a motorway service station at 6am one morning; she was lucky not to have been run over and despite the efforts of the local dog warden to track down her original owners, no one came forward to take responsibility for her, so she came to live with me.

Despite having a completely unknown history, Nancy seemed pretty cool, until she saw a bigger dog, which is when she went ballistic. Unfortunately for Nancy, *all* dogs are bigger dogs!

As Nancy came to me from the stray-dog pound where she'd been surrounded by other dogs, I wanted to make sure she had a bit of a 'cortisol holiday', when she first arrived. For a week or two we just stuck with low-octane, exploratory walks in areas and at times I knew we wouldn't meet other dogs. In addition to plenty of playing and affection to build trust and to establish our relationship, here are the exercises I taught Nancy that will also work for Polly should you ever be ambushed by a bigger dog and need some tools to help you get outta Dodge:

REFLEX TO NAME

See page 68 for how to train a reflex to name, which will act as 'power-steering'.

When faced with a potentially threatening situation, you'll need to get Polly's attention back on to you, without creating tension on the lead. Tension on the lead when faced with a threat tells Polly she no longer has her 'flight' option, leaving 'fight' the only card left to play.

Have you ever seen the guy being held back in the pub by his mates when it looks like a fight's about to start? More often than not the guy being restrained by his mates is doing all the shouting, 'Oh yeah, c'mon then!' Funnily enough, when his mates let him go, the guy tends to quieten a little and runs his fingers through his hair and straightens his collar, rather than 'giving it large'! I'm not saying let Polly go when faced with her nemesis, but use your reflex to name to get her to turn to you on a slack lead with no tension or restraint, rather than raising her head and chest to the other dog and restricting her 'flight' option.

EYE CONTACT

See pages 24–26 on how to teach eye contact.

Reflex to name is great when we see the other dog before Polly does, but what if Polly sees the other dog first? I want you to repeat your eye contact training in as many different locations as possible so it becomes a real default behaviour. We want Polly to trust that if there's something she wants, then she needs to look up to you and you'll provide. In some situations, she may want access to something, in others she may want removal from something she perceives as a potential threat.

'LET'S GO!'

We're putting together the tools of your training plan here but as Mike Tyson once said, 'Everyone has a plan until they get punched in the mouth!' It's important we have a secondary plan for such metaphorical punches in the mouth and that's going to be your 'Let's go!' cue. It may be that you're walking along the street and all of a sudden, a dog and owner appear out of nowhere and are heading straight towards you. You have no time to wait for Polly to do the right thing and the longer you wait, the closer the oncoming dog gets.

If in doubt, and for damage limitation, throw in a 'Let's go!' manoeuvre. Simply pat your leg, say nice and loud, 'Let's go!' and by hook or by crook, you turn 180 degrees, like a pigeon spotting a sleeping cat, then head off in the opposite direction away from the other dog, bringing Polly with you to make good your escape.

To practise, stand out in the garden with Polly on the lead, both of you facing the same direction. Out of the blue say, 'Let's go!', tap your thigh and then do an about turn, walk a couple of steps and heavily treat Polly as she comes with you. Repeat this exercise 20 times per session and practise in as many different locations to really proof the behaviour.

N.B. In every other exercise I ever teach, I never want to let the lead go tight; however, for this one exercise I make an exception. We need to prepare for what may happen when we go live. If you *are* caught unawares and another dog heads towards you and there's no time to wait for eye contact or throw in a reflex to name, the lead *is* going to go tight as you turn to make your getaway. If that happens, your multiple rehearsals of 'Let's go!' will teach Polly that when she hears those two words and the thigh pat, then even if the lead does go tight, it predicts GOOD news, not bad. The association we'll get is one of positive expectation, not 'fight' and dread. We'll be keeping her tolerance fuse nice and long. After several practices, Polly will soon cop on that the 'Let's go!' message simply means, *Turn quickly, there's good stuff behind Margaret!'*

The above exercises are your short-term 'in-case-of-emergency-break-glass' exercises and as long as you're aware of your surroundings when out and about with Polly, they will serve to keep you safe.

Your longer-term training will be geared towards desensitising Polly to the presence of other dogs. Desensitising means that Polly will be exposed to other dogs *that will be at a safe distance and posing no threat*, so she can get used to being comfortable in their presence. Over time and by carefully observing Polly's body language (see page 12) to ensure she's relaxed, you will gradually be able to reduce the proximity.

In addition, your long-term training will also include elements of counter-conditioning, which means when Polly sees another dog, good things happen. For example, you can stand with Polly then the second she spots another dog at a safe distance, you rain treats down upon her. When the other dog disappears, so do the treats.

Over time and with a lot of repetition, not only will Polly fist-pump and say 'Yes!' the second she sees another dog as a result of the successful positive associations you've made, but she'll also look up to you (eye contact) in anticipation of the treats: win-win!

Bringing it back to Nancy and me as a final, but important, point, the day I took her home to live with me, I made a contract with her – as I do with all of my dogs – and that is a simple promise: 'I'll keep you safe.'

'No matter what, I'll keep you safe, Nancy.'

That means if a dog's thundering towards her and we've no better option, too right I'm going to pick her up to keep her safe. If nothing else, I need Nancy to trust that if she ever feels like a situation is going to get on top of her, *I've got her back*. Once she knows I've got her back, she can relax, we can extend the fuse to the bomb. The responsibility is on *my* shoulders, not hers. If she ever felt I didn't have her back, that she had to ward off all potential scary dogs on her own, then she'd be a nervous wreck, looking to over-react at the slightest hint of danger. That's unhealthy and stressful.

You keep letting Polly know that you'll look after her no matter what, and give *her* the tools to help you do that. We're in the fuse-lengthening business now! And if anyone says you shouldn't pick up your dog, give them my number!

BARKING AT MEN

Hi Steve,

I live alone with my five-month-old puppy Ralph. He's normally a rather happy-go-lucky chap but seems to hate my neighbour Paul! The first time Paul came over, he went to stroke Ralph as he was lying in his basket and although he obviously wasn't too happy, as he just froze there, he seemed to tolerate the stroking okay.

However, the next time Paul visited, Ralph growled at him but Paul carried on stroking him and said that Ralph would soon get over it.

Now when Paul comes over, Ralph barks at him, even if Paul's on the other side of the room! I figure Ralph will eventually learn that Paul is friendly but I wanted to ask if this is the best route to take or should we consider something else? Paul is very committed to becoming friends with Ralph, so I'm sure whatever you suggest he'll be happy to put into practice.

Thank you!
Sally

Hi Sally,

Who knows why Ralph wasn't comfortable with Paul the first time they met. Perhaps Ralph hasn't met enough men yet in his short life; perhaps he was suffering from toothache the day Paul appeared and Ralph associated Paul's presence with the discomfort; perhaps Ralph had a bone under his bed and was afraid Paul was going to take it; or perhaps Ralph knows that deep down, Paul's really a cat-person.

Whatever the reason, it's important that Ralph understands that when he speaks politely, we listen.

When I say 'speak politely', what I mean is polite language – so the signals that say, 'No, thank you' or 'I'd rather you didn't'.

Ralph offered such a request when he 'froze' the first time Paul attempted to stroke him. Other polite signals to decline petting may be turning his head away, lowering his head or body posture, lip licking or yawning.

It's really, *really* important that Ralph trusts that we'll listen when he uses these polite requests from his vocabulary. If we don't, as is the case so far with Paul's interactions, it's like we're saying to Ralph, 'Nope, not listening, mate. Those words don't work, you're going to have to speak louder.'

'Louder' words in Ralph's vocabulary are going to be behaviours like lip-curling to ask Paul to back off, then if that doesn't work, Ralph may have to step it up to growling.

If that doesn't work, then Ralph may have to snap. It's at that point I'm often contacted by owners to be told that the dog 'bit the person out of the blue, with no warning!'

Let's not encourage Ralph to speak in CAPS LOCK.

We don't want to take words out of Ralph's vocabulary; if anything, we want to extend it by letting him know he doesn't have to resort to shouting. In addition to listening and responding to what Ralph needs, let's build a plan so he can meet Paul – and other men – without feeling stressed or afraid.

First up, meeting Paul in your house may be a little intense for Ralph as it's already been poisoned with the unpleasant meetings in the past, so we want to set up the positive meet-and-greets to be somewhere neutral, say the local park, where there's lots of space and Ralph won't feel restrained or with his 'back against the wall'.

A few tips below to help the next (and future meetings) with Paul go well:

- 🐾 Go at Ralph's pace.

- 🐾 Keep an eye on Ralph's body language to ensure he's comfortable and enjoying any interaction.

- 🐾 At first, just have Paul sat next to you as *you* treat and interact with Ralph.

- 🐾 Allow Ralph to approach Paul for treats, as opposed to Paul approaching Ralph.

- Keep the lead slack during introductions.

- Make sure that if at any point Ralph wants to disengage or retreat from Paul, he can.

- Less is more. Keep positive interactions short and sweet so Ralph is happy to see Paul the next time.

- Don't push your luck!

It's important to go slowly and to take one step at a time. Don't aim for a successful meeting to be Paul and Ralph rolling around on the floor like a cut scene from *Brokeback Mountain*; just aim for short, relaxed interactions with Ralph happily taking treats and maintaining a relaxed body posture.

As with all training, it's much better to steadily take one step forward at a time, rather than pushing your luck, having a negative experience and sliding down the ladder back to the start again.

Best of luck!

FIREWORKS

Hello Steve,

Our Dalmatian Dilly-Dally (named by my daughter, not me!) seems to have developed a real fear of fireworks recently. In previous years, she's been a little concerned but this last November 5th she got herself into a real state. Thankfully we live fairly remotely, so only have one local firework display a mile away from our home, so at least firework season isn't too long for us. She's three years of age and was actually spayed the day prior to this year's local display; we joked that hopefully the anaesthetic would last long enough to keep her dozy throughout the whizzes and bangs but actually quite the opposite happened, she was far more agitated than last time. Even though we tried to grab her to calm her down, she was pacing for ages, normally her obedience is excellent but asking her to 'Come' or 'Lie down' just fell on deaf ears. Eventually she began to dig the carpet by the settee like she was trying to bury herself. We tried to distract her with her favourite food but to our surprise she seemed repulsed by it! We don't want to molly-coddle her and reinforce the fear but to be honest, we're at a loss as to what we actually can do. Over to you!

Robert

Hi Robert,

The good news is, as always, there's tons you can do!

Fireworks season can be the most hideous time of year for many dogs. Thankfully you only have one display to prepare for each year; many built-up areas seem to have random firework attacks for weeks upon end. I hate being the Fun Police here but I despise fireworks. The amount of trauma it can cause, not just for dogs but for all domestic and farm animals, surely far outweighs the entertainment value ... Right, rant over, let's be proactive and positive, let's see how we can help Dilly-Dally (great name BTW!) and you.

A couple of threads to pick up on from your letter first that will assist you in prepping for next year's bombardment. Hoping that Dilly would be still zoned-out from her drugs after spaying was definitely some wishful thinking on your part. In fact, the reason she was more agitated this year may well be down to a process called *trigger-stacking*.

Trigger-stacking is when a stressful event is followed too soon by another, which in turn compounds the amount of stress the dog is under. The cumulative effect results in the dog (or any animal under similar stressors) reacting more intensely than if they faced the one individual stressor in isolation.

Imagine if you came home from work and your daughter

told you she'd lost her mobile phone; you may not be too pleased, but your reaction would be 'graded' appropriately to the event. Now imagine that you've had an awful day at work, in fact you've had a pay-cut (stressor one), traffic was murder on the way home (stressor two), you've a banging headache (stressor three) and to top it off someone's parked across your driveway when you eventually do make it home (stressor four). You then come indoors only to hear that your daughter has lost her mobile phone, 'ARRRGGGhhhhh!' I'm betting your response will be way above what would be considered reasonable on another day from someone of your good nature.

Us mammals, for good reason, are super-quick at kicking into our sympathetic 'fight or flight' programmes as a reaction to a stressor. The trouble is, our bodies are not so quick to get rid of hormones such as adrenalin and cortisol that spike in our bodies when faced with a perceived danger. It may take a good *36 hours* for those agitation-inducing hormones to dissipate. If we have layer upon layer of stressors put upon us over too short a time period, then our response to each following stressor will increase in intensity, our fuse gets shorter and shorter until ... BANG!

Let's take that as lesson one: in preparation for next year's fireworks display, make sure that Dilly has a good couple of chilled days leading up to the event, with plenty of exercise but no trauma, giving her every chance to keep that fuse as long as possible.

Lesson two: you mentioned that you tried to stop her pacing. It's important that when stressed, or at any other time for that matter, that dogs are allowed as much agency as is safely possible. If she needs to pace, she *needs* to pace. We know pacing can go some way to relieving stress; if it didn't, we wouldn't do it at the train station waiting for our sweetheart to (hopefully) turn up. Don't knock it, Hugh Grant's made a career out of it!

Lesson three? *Survival trumps obedience*, every time. Asking her to sit or lie down fell on 'deaf ears' because she was frightened for her life. Of course, the plan here is to help Dilly not get into such as a state, but if she ever does, let her find what little solace she can, however she can.

You mentioned that she tried to dig under the settee to escape the danger. That's not unusual, when dogs are scared they will try and go low to escape (cats will often attempt to go high). So, for next year you're going to build a den for Dilly, throw a couple of heavy blankets over the dining table and for the weeks leading up to November 5th you're going to show Dilly just how cool an area it is. The den is going to be where she can choose to enjoy her food, chews, even cuddles with you. Under you go, belly rubs and cuddles all round, it'll do you both good! It's important to introduce it as a cool place to hang out well before the fireworks start, so she knows exactly where to head should she decide to hide away in her safe place.

Right, let's get a plan together for next year...

DESENSITISATION

First things first ... last time Dilly proved 'sensitised' to the fireworks. We're going to help 'desensitise' Dilly by exposing her to an extremely low-level version of that stimulus, a level that's so low that initially she's only just aware of the sound and, importantly, not even slightly aroused by the noise. We're going to do this by playing a fireworks display on YouTube in the house at a super-low volume. It's really important here that you don't go too loud too soon. I'd much rather you play it so quiet that Dilly can't even hear it then progressively turn it up over the following days, weeks and months, rather than blow the whole process out of the water by being too greedy for progress early on. Remember, a dog's hearing is so much more acute than ours, so *ear* on the side of caution. I thank you!

If next year's fireworks night is the best part of a year away, then when should you start your desensitisation programme? As with all dog training, the best time to start is *now*. If Dilly looks completely unimpressed, good, that's what we're after. Start the process in the mornings, so it's as removed as possible from the negative experience she had this year. Over the following weeks, raise the volume by 0.5 at a time, no rush to get to the end. The value is in laying the solid foundation and preparing well in advance. As Lincoln said, 'If you have eight hours to chop down a tree, spend six hours sharpening the axe.'

After several weeks, once you're up to full blast and if it's logistically possible, make it more realistic by having your laptop or speakers on the windowsill or behind the curtains and building up the volume again from there. Then repeat the build-up behind the curtain, but at night-time.

If *at any stage* Dilly looks the slightest bit concerned, no worries, go back to volume one and start the build-up again. That's the beauty of starting months in advance, you can adapt the training plan to Dilly, not the other way around.

And remember, you're lucky you've got 'firework display' sounds at your fingertips via YouTube 24/7 nowadays. Pull up a chair young 'un ... When I was 15, I had to traipse down to our local library and rent the BBC Sound Effects vinyl albums (at 20p for two weeks, if you don't mind!), record them onto tape so I didn't have to keep re-renting them (I wasn't made of money), and then use those for my desensitisation programmes. Cool albums though: pneumatic drills, traffic, crowds cheering, fireworks, audiences booing ... all the big hits were on those albums. My school friends were going to discos and chatting up girls for dating purposes. I was recording the sound of church bells onto a Maxell cassette for dog training purposes.

COUNTER-CONDITIONING

At the moment, Dilly has a fear response to fireworks. We're going to turn that frown upside down. We can bring a bit more to the party by pairing the YouTube firework sounds with access to things that Dilly likes.

Hear that Whizz? Have some cheese!
Bang? No biggie, here's some ham!
Pop! Yes! Chicken time!

Be generous with the treats when the video is playing and make sure you stop the treats as soon as the video stops. That way Dilly can appreciate the relationship between the two events.

So, the local fireworks event is looming, you've done all of the hard yards of desensitisation and counter-conditioning. On the day itself, shift everything forward a little so she gets her exercise and evening meal nice and early in daylight hours. Have the curtains drawn, the TV up nice and loud like an old-people's home and relax. You mentioned that you don't want to 'molly-coddle' Dilly but here's the deal: if she needs such comfort, bloody give it to her! You 100% *will not* reinforce her fear or make her any worse by comforting her. You're a family; if she needs you, be there for her. Imagine being afraid *and* being blanked by your best mate, no way. You have my permission to molly-coddle to your heart's content; in fact, I insist! If she does have to go out into the garden in the dark, you *must* go out with her, armed with a bagful of treats. If a bang does go off, make sure you get that treat into her quick-smart to confirm that fireworks predict good news. Don't spend any longer than you need to outside in the dark; a quick tinkle then back indoors again where you've got your lovely den, food, toys, chews and a loud TV waiting.

When she was frightened this year, you mentioned that she didn't eat, that's because the 'fight or flight' response can actually supress the appetite. That's the body's way of saying '*I can't afford to waste energy on digestion, I might need all my energy to fight or run for my life here, snacking can wait!*' Because you've put in the desensitisation groundwork, that fear won't be present, so she'll be able to enjoy her bounty. Even if she is feeling slightly concerned, access to chewing will help Dilly release nice, relaxing endorphins into her brain. Other ideas include considering the use of a plug-in DAP (Dog Appeasing Pheromone) diffuser which replicates the calming pheromones that a mother emits to her puppies. In extreme cases, talk to your vet to discuss supporting medications available.

So, there you go. Spend the next few months 'sharpening your axe' and you'll breeze through November 5th. Enjoy working through the process, do it slowly and Dilly will love you all the more for it!

SEPARATION ANXIETY

Dear Steve,

My dog Holly gets so upset when we go out. My dog trainer says it's separation anxiety and that she'll get over it. She has suggested leaving a radio on when we go out; however, I now actually hate the thought of going out if no one else is home, I can't stand the fact that she's going to be so stressed. We've had her since she was a pup, she's six years of age now and up until last autumn she used to be fine being left alone. She's recently had a vet check and nothing else in her day-to-day life has changed, same diet, exercise, etc. that she's always had.

She's definitely getting worse as I've noticed she now paces when I'm even thinking about getting ready to go out, and if I'm the only one in the house with her it feels like she's watching me intently almost 24/7. I live with my two adult sons and if either of them, or their girlfriends, are with Holly, she's fine. It's just when she's on her own that she seems to panic. Over the last couple of months there's been times I've had to resort to sneaking out of the house via the back door so she doesn't notice my departure, but each time I've returned she's seemed very stressed and my neighbours (who are lovely, thankfully!) have mentioned that they've heard her whining and barking intermittently. We've had to replace the carpet by the living room door where she frantically scratches.

Please help, I hate to see her like this and I'm not sure what to do.

Best,
Susan

Hi Susan,

Ah, that's so tough on you all. I really feel for dogs (and owners) suffering from separation anxiety. Let's take this letter as the first step in getting you all back on track and building a training plan that's going to seem long, but worthwhile.

Over many generations we've selectively bred domestic dogs for the looks, working skill-set and social 'stickability' that we, as owners, enjoy. Unfortunately, some dogs place such high value on the need to be with their family that any separation can be extremely stressful for them, leading to whining and barking, destruction, incontinence, in fact a whole plethora of stress-fuelled behaviours. 'Separation Anxiety', 'Separation Distress', 'Hyper-Attachment' ... the problem comes with several labels, but let's look at how we can help build Holly's confidence and maybe even allow her to enjoy a little bit of 'me time'.

First up, separation anxiety can be present for different reasons:

Separation: This is when the dog becomes stressed when separated from a *specific* person. Other people may still be present and accessible by the dog, but they just cannot relax until reunited with that one special person.

Isolation: In any location, the dog becomes stressed when left alone in isolation. If the dog has company, anyone friendly, they can cope.

Conditioned Fear: This is when, during a past episode when left alone in a specific area, the dog experienced a fright such as thunder or fireworks. The dog puts 'two and two together' and deduces that *when left alone here, scary stuff happens creating panic and anxiety in this location.* Anxiety being the fear of fear. Something scary *might* happen.

The fact that Holly used to be okay, but has now started getting stressed when she suspects she's about to be left alone at home, coupled with the fact that she's OK as long as someone, anyone, is with her, plus the fact that it started early November – firework season – means that all fingers point to conditioned fear. Of course, these may all be red herrings but I'd be willing to bet that's the track we're on.

You mentioned that Holly has now started pacing when you're getting ready to go out and if you're the only one with her that she stares intently at you. Obviously, they're signs that she's worried about being left home alone, but the increase in her vigilance will be fuelled by the few times you've 'sneaked' out of the back door to go out. I absolutely appreciate why you felt the need to do this; however, it will have put even more unpredictability into Holly's world. She's become hyper-vigilant; the only way you'll sneak out of the house now is up the chimney or down the toilet! The good news is I don't want you being a sneaky ninja anymore; we're going to add more predictability into Holly's world, not suspicion.

The vocalisation your neighbours mention is certainly not uncommon with separation anxiety cases. Distress calling is just some of the software automatically uploaded into puppies during the juvenile stages that serves a survival purpose because when the mother hears the distress call, she's able to locate her offspring and return them to safety. With separation anxiety, the vocalisation is often, as you say, intermittent. That's because its purpose is to try and trigger a call-response routine: 'Hello? Hello, anyone there? ... *(silence, desperately waiting for a response)* ... Hello? ... you seem to have locked me in the house by mistake ... can you hear me? ... Help! ... Help!'

I wonder if you ever notice any of these other signs upon your return to a Home Alone Holly?

- Chewing: perhaps with a particular focus around certain exit/entrance hotspots such as doorways or windows?

- Anorexia: does Holly refuse to eat when she suspects she's about to be left or during your absence?

- Incontinence while you're absent?

- Drool: when you return to your home, can you see any signs of drool on the floor, perhaps near the window or door where Holly may have waited for you, barking or panting?

Be aware, just like us, that some dogs are extroverts, others are introverts. Some people will scream and shout when upset, others will turn in on themselves, go unusually quiet and shut down. Just because dog 'A' isn't as vocal as dog 'B' when left alone, doesn't necessarily mean they are suffering any less. Watch for tell-tale body language such as tight posture, wide eyes, or other signs of distress such as panting or pacing.

All of these *may* be signs of separation anxiety but there may be perfectly reasonable alternative reasons why these symptoms are occurring. That's why, when I am presented with a case, it's important that I run through any potential 'rule-outs' before digging into a heavier behaviour modification programme. For example, perhaps the chewing is simply teething relief or boredom when left alone? Perhaps the incontinence is evidence that the toilet training wasn't quite as 'on point' as the owners thought, or hoped, it was?

As pain and discomfort are the most common causes of sudden behaviour changes, it is great that Holly has had a full vet check-up and that she's medically all clear. With that confirmed, we can get to work.

The training programme for dealing with separation anxiety is unfortunately going to feel fairly prescriptive and pretty involved, but there's plenty of easy wins that you can start training for right now that will make the whole process as effective as possible.

REHAB PREPARATION

Ideally, until she's ready, I would not want Holly to be left alone at home for periods of time that she's unable to cope with. To help facilitate this, recruit a crack back-up team of family, friends and neighbours that you can bully, cajole, blackmail or bribe into sitting with Holly in times of need.

Aside from the exercises detailed on the following pages, build Holly's confidence and independence by ensuring she has pleasant and relaxed experiences *away* from you. You can do this by scatter-feeding in the garden. Simply throw a handful of her daily food or treat allowance into the back garden and allow her to go off and have a good old snuffle around while you stay in the kitchen with the back door open. It's important at this stage that if she wants to rejoin you or simply just check-in to make sure you're still around, she absolutely can. The food scattering must not be used as a trick to trap her away from you, because the whole process is about building **faith, trust and confidence**, not suspicion. Scatter-feeding is merely a vehicle to demonstrate to Holly that she can be away from you, *and* have a jolly good time while she's at it!

THE TRAINING TARGET

Allow Holly to comfortably learn that being on her own in the house is fine. The training exercises will take the form of a three-pronged attack: 'Distance', 'Settle' and 'Chill-Out'. We'll work on each 'prong' individually but concurrently, and when all are up-to-speed, we'll weave them together for our holistic approach. Bear with me, it's detailed, but this is too important an issue to go half measures. Holly deserves the best.

Exercise One: Distance

For this, we're going to teach down as normal (see pages 59–67), but have a real emphasis on building distance and duration, eventually with you being able to go out of sight for longer and longer durations of time, while allowing Holly to remain relaxed, comfortable and optimistic. Initially, practise in as many different locations as possible to really proof the behaviour, then build up to being able to cue Holly into a down before walking away from her and disappearing out of sight for a good 30 seconds. This is a great formal foundation for our other exercises and reinforces that moments away from you can have positive associations. During training, always wear your *Safety Signal*. Intrigued? More about a *Safety Signal* to come later!

Exercise Two: Settle

The Settle Mat: I want Holly to learn she has her very own safe spot to relax in. Check out our settle chapter on pages 174–9 to find out how to build a target area for relaxation. Once Holly has learned the mental and physical comfort awaiting on her settle mat, and because of the many repetitions of Exercise One above, she'll soon start offering a down on her mat, which we can then introduce to Exercise Three below.

Exercise Three: Chill-Out

Creating the Chill-Out Zone: this is ultimately where you will be leaving Holly for her Home Alone sessions when you do eventually have to go out. That's in the future though. For now, we're just going to illustrate to her just how cool an area it is. As you mentioned that Holly has obviously been stressed in the living room when left alone (as evidenced by the scratched carpet), that area may well be 'poisoned' now, so ideally let's use a different location, a new blank canvas to start building positive associations with. It's more effective to start from zero and build up a nice positive balance, rather than start from minus 100. No one wants to work just to pay off a debt. So, our new chill-out zone will be your kitchen.

A few days prior to training this exercise, I recommend you fit a child gate across your kitchen door. This will help Holly to accept the boundary aspect of staying in the kitchen and also certainly help with the later stages of increasing your distance from her. I'd like you to fit the child gate a few days prior to the training, so she can become appropriately comfortable with its presence.

Over the next couple of weeks, work through the stages gradually as per below, only moving on to the next stage, when you're sure she's comfortable with the current one:

1. Prepare the chill-out zone. Don't let Holly into the kitchen just yet. You go in first and scatter plenty of great treats around, leave a few nice toys and make sure the settle mat is in there. (The settle mat won't play a part in the safe area process just yet, but I want it in the picture for later and you know what, if she *does* leapfrog our training plan and jumps straight on to settling, I'll take that!).

   When you're ready, open the gate and let Holly in to find all the goodies. This stage is designed to give a good association with the area. You stay in with Holly, but stay passive. It's the location that we want Holly's focus to be on.

   Work through this process a couple of times

a day for a good few days. No rush. We're better off going through the whole process slowly and smoothly once from start to finish rather than having to rewind and repeat elements.

Slow is smooth and smooth is fast.

1. As per above but on a few sessions, do a little settle mat training in the chill-out zone. Nothing too much, just enough to put the settle mat into context and to remind Holly that chilling on the mat pays dividends.

   Every now and then do a few down repetitions. Combine a few short downs with the settle mat. Again, nothing too adventurous, just a few short bonus sessions to start blending the three training 'prongs' together.

2. Start to enter the prepared area with Holly and, as she roams around, you can open the gate and simply stand on the other side, closing the gate between the two of you. She'll no doubt look up but as she'll still be able to see you, she'll be fine. She'll soon get back to enjoying the treasure on the kitchen floor! Over several sessions, build up the duration you're on the other side of the gate away from her.

3. As you've been working on your distance training of downs concurrently, you will now be able to start leaving Holly in the kitchen on the other side of the gate while you start adding distance between the pair of you. There's no requirement to ask Holly for a down here, it's the distance and duration elements you've been training for that are the active ingredients we need; the position of down has just acted as a tool to get you to this point. Allow Holly to happily mooch around the chill-out zone as you leave. Gradually be out of sight for 10 seconds before calmly returning, then 20, then 30, then a few minutes. It's important that sometimes you return *after* Holly has finished all the treats. It's also important that she actually *does* realise you're not there. We're doing these repetitions to build resilience to being left alone. We're not trying to sneak away when she's not looking. Sneaking away creates unpredictability, unpredictability creates suspicion and suspicion creates anxiety.

4. Before you work through this stage, I'd like you to write down your leaving routine. For example, imagine it's something like: put shoes on; grab coat from cloakroom; take car keys from hallway table; open front door; leave.

If that's so, then that's the routine you're going
to start building into this stage, layer by layer. It's
important that you keep your leaving routine as
simple, predictable and consistent as possible. No
long drawn out, 'I'm going now' (as you look under
the settee for your left shoe), 'Here I go, love you'
(as you cartwheel past the kitchen door looking for
your car keys) ... 'See you, this is me leaving' (as you
climb the chandelier looking for your right shoe) ...
'Off I go ...', etc.

Be consistent, be predictable, but don't leave
Holly hovering at the amber light forever. This
stage will look like the early stages of Exercise
Two, in the respect that you're letting Holly into
the chill-out zone without asking her to do any
specific behaviour, combined with Exercise One,
as you gradually increase distance (but this time
with no formal down), layer by layer adding extra
elements of your leaving routine before heading
back into the chill-out zone to rejoin Holly.

Over the next week or so, a cross-section of your
training stages should look something like:

... Step 6 ... release Holly into chill-out zone, leave
area, walk to shoe cupboard, pick up shoes, return
to Holly in the chill-out zone.

... Step 13 ... release Holly into chill-out zone, leave area, walk to shoe cupboard, pick up shoes, sit on bottom stair and put on shoes, walk to cloakroom, put on coat, pick up car keys from hallway table ... return to Holly in chill-out zone.

... Step 19 ... release Holly into chill-out zone, leave area, walk to shoe cupboard, pick up shoes, sit on bottom stair and put on shoes, walk to cloakroom, put on coat, pick up car keys from hallway table ... open front door (stay inside), close door, return to Holly...

... Step 22 ... release Holly into chill-out zone, leave area, walk to shoe cupboard, pick up shoes, sit on bottom stair and put on shoes, walk to cloakroom, put on coat, pick up car keys from hallway table, open front door ... go outside, close door behind you, immediately return to Holly...

... Step 24 ... release Holly into chill-out zone, leave area, walk to shoe cupboard, pick up shoes, sit on bottom stair and put on shoes, walk to cloakroom, put on coat, pick up car keys from hallway table, open front door, go outside, close door behind you ... stay outside for 10 seconds, return to Holly...

... Step 26 ... release Holly into chill-out zone, leave area, walk to shoe cupboard, pick up shoes, sit on bottom stair and put on shoes, walk to cloakroom, put on coat, pick up car keys from hallway table, open front door, go outside, close door behind you ... stay outside for 30 seconds, then return to Holly ... and so on.

Please note: don't *always* add more and more for each repetition. Every now and then do a short period of time away. Sometimes 30 seconds, followed by 10 seconds, followed by two minutes, followed by five minutes, followed by 30 seconds, etc. When we're building 'duration away', we're best to zig-zag the length of our absences to consolidate and build resilience.

> ### IMPORTANT ANNOUNCEMENT: BEWARE OF THE CREEPY WALK!
>
> People walk naturally. Normally, almost like humans. That is *until* it's dog training time! Make sure that when you're wandering around in the chill-out zone and you then begin your leaving routine, don't start doing a Weird Creepy Walk! This is when you're trying just too hard to walk normally, giving it the whole 'Dum de dum, nothing to concern you here,

Holly, I'm just definitely walking normally! Definitely not trying to creep away like some Child Catcher!' Relax, WALK NORMALLY!

We need to make sure Holly LOVES these sessions. The start of each session must be seen as the start of something wonderful, a signal that only good news is on its way. We're doing this for Holly by building the duration of settle, distance and chill-out zone in nice small, manageable and successful increments but most importantly, we're lavishing each session with tons of rewards. This serves two purposes: not only does it helps us reinforce the behaviours we want more of such as the settle, but more important than that, we're pairing 'time alone' with only good things. We're changing the emotional response of how Holly feels about being left alone, and in so doing, we're changing her world for the better.

This all looks great on paper, doesn't it?! Simple. Step One leads to Step Two leads to Step Three and Hey Presto! We have a happy Holly! Unfortunately, life gets in the way sometimes and despite your best efforts of not leaving Holly alone for longer periods than she can cope with, an emergency outing may be needed and you just don't have the chance to arrange for one of your 'crack support squad' of family members or neighbours to come in and sit with her. If possible and it's safe to do so, bring Holly with you; early on in the programme, dogs are often more content in the car than being left alone at home, especially in 'conditioned fear' cases like this one for Holly. (If the car is an option, make sure she's never in there for too long, and that she's safe, secure and comfortable.)

If it's just not possible to have her with you on the trip, we need to prep for a damage-limitation mode, we need a signal to Holly that says, 'I'm sorry mate, I know it's tough, but I gotta go.' If we're going to be forced to take a backwards step in our progress, I want that step to be as small as possible, with as little an amount of damage to our training programme as we can get away with.

That's where our 'Safety Signal' comes in, as I mentioned earlier. Bear with me, I admit it's a little odd…

You're going to condition your safety signal as per below *before* you do any of the three training exercises above. (I've left it until now to describe the process because I didn't want to freak you out too early!)

Let's say your safety signal is *a baseball cap.*

From the very first training session to the last, wear your cap EVERY SINGLE TIME as a rock-solid guarantee to Holly that you're not going to leave her any longer than she can cope with.

The cap will help us avoid suspicion *and*, because you're generous with the reinforcement, it will predict that good times are coming.

Start by conditioning the fact that the baseball cap predicts good news for Holly:

Put cap on = treat, treat, treat
Take cap off = stop treats
Put cap on = treat, treat, treat
Take cap off = stop treats

Do this in several locations at several times throughout the day. The behaviour that Holly does is irrelevant, the only thing she needs to be able to say to herself is:

When the cap is on, everything's good and everything's safe!
I LOVE it when the cap is on.
I wish Mum wasn't naked, but still, the cap is on,
I can forgive!

When you start to observe happy, anticipatory body language from Holly, such as a relaxed wagging tail or clear expectant eyes when she sees you put your cap on, you can then start the distance downs, the settle and chill-out zone training as per above. *At the beginning of each session, the cap goes on.* The training starts, the good times roll and the positive associations begin. At the end of the session, the cap comes off.

IF YOU CAN'T AVOID LEAVING HOLLY BEFORE SHE'S READY

The cap now acts as a safety signal to Holly that only good things are coming, that she's not going to be pushed beyond her limits. With the safety signal now in place, if you *do* unavoidably need to go out and you know Holly has to be left Home Alone and possibly pushed beyond her limits, it sucks, but **just don't put the cap on** before you go out.

This is a way of underwriting your training sessions, a way for you to smooth out the potential speed bumps you may hit along the way of your rehabilitation journey for the unavoidable times you have to leave her. A way to avoid poisoning training sessions. A way to upload extra predictability.

The cap is an insurance.

Note: Once you're able to leave the house for longer periods of time during training sessions, perhaps get in the habit of taking your cap off and leaving it outside by the front door when you depart and popping it back on when you return to Holly. There's no need for you to continually wear your cap at the coffee shop or the cinema. You're not American.

There is no point in me pretending that helping a dog with separation anxiety isn't a really tough one, so don't be afraid to recruit the technical and moral support of a good professional dog trainer or vet. There are other simple, practical things you can think about. Maybe consider the use of a plug-in DAP diffuser which emits Dog Appeasing Pheromones that may help with the training. Turning a radio on for Holly can also help break the deadly silence of being Home Alone, but don't only put it on if you're going out. We don't want it to become a signal that being solitary is imminent. Also consider her exercise routine – sometimes dogs are more relaxed after a walk, but sometimes they might seem more 'revved up'.

It's a long process and the journey back to where you want to be may seem some distance away, perhaps even a few months, but don't rush. *Do it properly and do it once.* There'll be a few blips but the safety signal will limit any threatening negative effects. Once your training is gathering speed and you're starting to go out of sight from Holly, consider the use of a video camera set-up that you can see on your phone to ensure her body language remains comfortable and that you're not pushing her too far too soon.

Like all of us, there'll be times when Holly feels confident and bold, and there'll be times when she'll feel insecure and delicate. That's okay, she's only human, cut your cloth accordingly and you'll see progress over the days, weeks and months.

Learning is never in a straight line but rest assured: it's worth the effort, *you're making her life better.*

For any of the above stages, if Holly shows signs of stress or concern, simply go back a stage or two and consolidate. A positive association is what's most important here, not trying to 'weather the storm' whilst keeping our fingers crossed! This is science people, no need for hit and hope!

PART 3
EXERCISES FOR QUALITY OF LIFE

There's living with your dog, then there's reeeally living with your dog! This section is all about the ways you and your dog can live your best life. I've included exercises to engage the nose of your dog and the brains of both of you! Enrichment exercises for daily nourishment as well as exercises to build trust and to tap into the phenomenal tools only a dog possesses.

TRICKS

Hello Steve,

Myself, my brother, my mum and my dad all live happily with our four rescue dogs, and as part of our family's New Year's resolution, we've promised to spend more constructive time having fun and training with our dogs. We've all decided that we'll train with a different individual dog each month and the first Sunday of every month we'll have a 'Dog-Off', with the winning team being the one that has best mastered a new trick. My dad was a little resistant to the idea of teaching tricks as opposed to normal training but the majority vote won! By the end of the year we're hoping we'll have well-trained happy dogs, and 48 new tricks up our sleeves to maybe write our own dog training book to compete with yours!

So, what we want from you is the first four tricks we can start teaching to get the ball rolling for us, please.

Thank you!

Kirsty, Paul, Malcolm, Ann, Rolo, Trooper, Jasmine & Fox! (aka The Martin Family)

Hello Team Martin,

Competitive much?!

I think a monthly Dog-Off is a lovely idea to increase quality time spent with the dogs – good for you! Tell your dad that as far as dogs are concerned, it's all tricks to them! I'm very happy to offer a few tricks below BUT (stern Mum's voice), the rules for teaching any dog tricks are:

- It must be beneficial to the dog
- Only teach a movement that a dog could, and would, do naturally
- No over-use of the trick that could cause physical strains.

As with all training, it's really important we ask ourselves, *why* we're doing it, not just *how*. The 'why' is the benefit, not only to us, but also, crucially, to the dog.

Why should we teach it?
Why should we teach it this particular way?
Why should the dog do it?

Of course, any training using positive reinforcement and set at an appropriate level should offer all parties an opportunity for fun, bonding and learning, so if we stick to our stern Mum rules above, I'm going to suggest 'Spin', 'Bow', 'Leg Weaves' and, for our *pièce de résistance*, 'Peek-a-Boo'!

SPIN

'Spin' is a good exercise to teach as it helps the dog maintain flexibility, as well as being a cheeky little exercise you can throw into your loose lead walking training to keep your dog on their toes and listening for the next cue. It's important when we're teaching spin, or any exercise for that matter, that we don't do an excessive amount of repetitions in one direction, without balancing out the repetitions in the other direction. Too many repetitions going anti-clockwise, for example, can easily cause a bias in the dog's muscular development leading to physical issues later. To that end, make sure you do an even amount of spins/twists in each direction. I use the verbal cue 'Spin' for anti-clockwise turns and the verbal cue 'Twist' for clockwise turns.

Start facing each other with the dog standing in front of you. Imagine you're both stood on a clock dial, with the dog's nose and your feet over the 6.

🐾 Hold a treat in your left hand and lower it down so it's level with the dog's nose. Slowly lure your dog's head anti-clockwise from 6 o'clock to 3 o'clock and, when in position, say 'Good' – and here's a sneaky tip – rather than placing the treat into the dog's mouth, throw the treat towards the 12 o'clock area. That way, the dog will already be practising a fluid movement in the correct direction and, if you're lucky, once you say 'Good' and throw the treat, you'll be getting 3 o'clock to 12 o'clock for free!

At this stage always start with your dog facing you and always make sure that you don't start luring the dog's head around until your hand is *level* with their nose. This is really important as often handlers do the luring motion above the dog's head, which results in the dog stretching upwards and doing a weird flippy, twisty movement. This not only looks ri-dic-u-lous dharling, but also risks injury.

- Again, starting from 6 o'clock, lower your treat-laden left hand down to the dog's nose and slowly lure the head around from 6 o'clock round to 12 o'clock, say 'Good' and grab your bonus track by throwing the treat around to 9 o'clock.

- Now you're ready to lure all the way around from 6 to 6, say 'Good', and throw the treat around to 3 o'clock in readiness for your second lap.

- Once the behaviour is nice and fluent, do exactly the same but say 'Spin' just before your lure from 6 to 6.

- Now to fade the lure.

  Hold your hand down to the dog's nose as before but have no treat in your hand, say 'Spin', complete the circle with your dog following your hand, then say 'Good', and take a treat from your pouch for your superstar.

- You may have noticed that as you move your left hand at your dog's nose height to complete the anti-clockwise circle, you step forward a little with your right foot so you can streeeeetch your arm to the furthest point of the circle, especially if your dog's a large breed and you're not! That's fine, the little step forward acts as an additional visual cue for your dog and will help us as we now look to minimise the hand signal.

Say 'Spin' and lure the dog's head around in the circle, and reward as before. On the next repetition, make your hand circle a little more subtle but feel free to step forward with your right foot again if necessary to reassure your dog they're on the right track as you say 'Spin'.

Because you've put in plenty of repetitions at the correct hand-to-nose height up to this stage, and because the behaviour is now on a nice reliable verbal cue, you can begin to gradually fade your hand signal into the background. Once your dog can spin with just a verbal cue and a subtle hand gesture, you can begin to give the cue from a distance and not have to have the arms of Mr Tickle to pull it off!

Twist

To teach 'Twist', simply have the treat in your *right* hand; lure the dog's head from 6 to 9 o'clock, 6 to 12 o'clock, 6 to 3 o'clock then all the way clockwise, 6 to 6 o'clock.

Use the verbal cue 'Twist' and step forward with your left foot. Remember, once trained, match your number of spins with twists to avoid imbalance.

BOW

Not only does 'Bow' look good, it has fantastic health benefits also. Like a banana. Along with spin and twist, asking your dog to do a few bows before any robust exercise session is a great way to warm up the body to help prevent any soft tissue injuries.

Away from training, dogs will sometimes bow as part of their morning stretch routine, especially sight hounds:

they'll wake up, bow down to stretch their front legs and chest, stretch out their back legs, stretch out their neck, yawn, then if they're anything like my Greyhound, they'll pop back on the sofa for another snooze. Rome wasn't built in a day, you know!

Dogs will also bow as an invite to other dogs to induce a game of chase. To avoid any confusion, they'll lower the pointy bitey end of their body to the ground, and raise their sassy, play-barging butt in the air for all to see. It's how I met my wife.

Follow these steps below to build the necessary components for a killer Bow:

🐾 For comfort, I recommend you start teaching this exercise with you sat on the floor and the dog facing you. With a treat in your closed fist, slowly slide your hand along the floor between your dog's two front feet. As your hand continues to slide along the ground below their chin and towards their chest, you'll notice their elbows and chest drop towards the floor. The second you see that lowering of the front end with their butt still in the air, say, 'Good!', lift your hand up and place the treat into their mouth with the dog ideally in a stand.

The reason I want you to feed the treat off the floor is so you can interrupt the downward momentum prior to the butt touching the floor and the dog therefore thinking the reinforcement is coming for a down, rather than a bow. If the dog does actually assume the down position after you say 'Good', no biggie, still give them the treat – a deal's a deal – just try and be a little sharper with your timing and delivery next time. Don't do too many repetitions, especially early on. Remember this is a fairly unique position so will take its toll on the body's core strength.

* Next step is to add a little more definite movement to each repetition, to progress from a slight lowering of the chest through to the desired bow position over the next few sessions. Make sure you layer the increase of movement over a series of sessions. Don't be too greedy too soon, as your dog will need to build up their core strength and you want to make sure they realise the lesson is to bow, not to collapse into a down.

   If your dog does keep dropping their hips, go back to reinforcing smaller increments of them lowering their chest from a stand position and make sure you reinforce them in any position but a down.

* In the future, we want to be able to ask the dog to do the behaviour, even if there's no food in our

hands. That's why at this stage, we're ready to fade the lure. Do the above, but with an empty fist. When your dog bows, say 'Good' and go with them to grab a treat from the pouch on a nearby table. This is a great method to bypass the dog going into a full down when you want to start adding duration to the position.

* Now you can start adding the verbal cue: say 'bow', slide your hand between their feet and, as they bow, say 'Good' and reinforce.

* Say 'bow' and begin to fade the hand signal between their feet. Use the closed fist a little less after each successful repetition until your dog is bowing purely on the verbal cue. Once the behaviour is on the verbal cue, you can ask your dog to bow with you in a standing position and at ever-increasing distances from you.

There you go, that's spin, twist and bow in the bag for you. Let's have a look at the 'Leg Weaves'...

LEG WEAVES

Leg weaves are a nice halfway house for us to borrow a little from your spin training above, and to prepare us for the future 'Peek-a-Boo' training below. On top of the additional flexibility benefits, it again keeps your loose-lead training interesting and really encourages your dog to get nice and close into you, which can only be of benefit for recalls.

- Start with your dog on your left-hand side, and take a big old step out with your right leg, placing it on the ground a metre or so in front of your left. With your feet planted, hold a treat with your right hand and lure your dog between your legs. As soon as your dog's shoulders have passed your right calf, say 'Good', and make sure your dog sees you slowly throw their treat forwards across the front of your right shin so they can practise a nice tight turn around your leg to get the goodies.

- Practise the above several times, then repeat the process but with the dog starting on your right-hand side, stepping forward with your left leg and luring through with your left hand. Remember to throw the treat across your shin once your dog's shoulders have passed your calf. It's these tight turns that are going to be the thread we need to stitch our left leg and right leg weaves together.

- Now the bit where you forget how to walk! Have a treat in both hands. With the dog on your left-hand side, step forward with your right leg, lure the dog through with your right hand and as soon as your dog's shoulders brush the back of your right calf, step forward with your left leg, pick up your dog's attention with the treat in your left hand, lure them behind your left calf, and around in front of your left shin as you throw the treat out to your right. Phew!

- Once the above 'two steps per treat' are smooth, progress to three, then four, then five steps per treat. You can then dispose of the treats in your hand and simply reinforce with a 'Good' and treat from your pocket once you hit the desired criteria, or a throw of the ball across your body if you want to add some speed and urgency into the proceedings to really funk it up!

PEEK-A-BOO

The finished article of a 'Peek-a-Boo' looks like this: you're standing, legs akimbo, with the dog stood or sat between your legs, facing in the same direction as you. This one's loaded with benefits as it makes the ears, eyes and mouth nice and easy to inspect and clean. Also, it's a fantastically controlled position to put your dog in if you're waiting in a restricted area such as a vet's surgery, or you want to keep your dog securely contained should you find yourself in the presence of unruly kids or someone that's not so confident around dogs.

- Stand like your favourite superhero with your legs astride, your hands on your hips and your gaze, steely, off into the distance... Now, grow up and focus.

  Hands off hips, eyes on the prize but legs can remain in the superhero stance. With your dog behind you, hold a few liver treats between your legs, like an offal sporran, and bend forward to encourage your dog to poke their head between your legs so you're both facing the same direction.

  As soon as their head is between your legs, feed them several treats individually, one at a time, so you can 'feed in position' and build the duration of them being in the right place at the right time.

  After feeding in position for a while, throw a treat out in front of you for your dog to get, turn your back on your dog so you can re-set and encourage your dog into position again for another repetition.

- Once your dog is fluently getting back in between your legs for each re-set, you can start to add the cue. With your back to your dog and your legs spread, say 'Peek-a-boo', encourage your dog to poke their head between your legs and feed in position.

🐾 Now you can start to add duration. With your dog in position, wait three seconds before reinforcing, then five seconds, then 10...

🐾 To really funk it up (and more importantly, to scoop gold at the inaugural Martin Family International Dog-Off), as your dog approaches from behind, turn your toes in towards each other pigeon-fashion, to create a little platform for your dog to place their own feet on to. This may take a little time and by all means you can use a treat to lure them into position. Initially, be happy with successfully placing one foot, then aim for the second. Once your dog is confidently placing a foot on each of your own feet, you can begin to take tiny steps together, like a dad teaching his daughter to waltz. Next stop, *Strictly*.

Enjoy your training, and enjoy your dog-off, sounds like fun!

SCENTWORK

Hiya Steve,

I've recently adopted a lovely three-legged Labrador called Pablo who's a very loving, energetic boy. However, at the moment he's not great with other dogs and we're working on this. Although he loves to run around exploring to burn off energy, he often trots up lame the morning after a big run due to missing a 'wheel'! When he was put into rescue by his previous owner, he was extremely overweight which we're slowly trying to chip away at. We've done a lot of basic training but I just want to know if there's any particular sport or activity you could suggest that we do together that doesn't require too much athleticism, yet still burns up his boundless energy and that we can do away from other dogs. He seems up for anything but, unfortunately, I can't just let him chase squirrels all day!

Thanks in advance,
Sue (and the squirrels!)

Hi Sue,

Pablo sounds cool!

Too often in our society we live with dogs that are over-fed and yet under-nourished.

The answer to your question is one word: SCENTWORK!

For *all* dogs, the opportunity to use their nose is an essential outlet for mental release, it makes them feel good, it's how they 'see' the world and, let's be honest, they're bloomin' good at it!

A dog's nose will never stop fascinating me. Even in my dog-handling days, I was privileged to be the 'student' to so many canine 'teachers'. I've worked with dogs in Africa that we trained to search and find the *scat* – poop in layman's terms – of predators such as cheetahs in order to collect important data on what they eat, where they go and how to protect the local livestock. In my security days, I've been saved more than once by my dog using their nose to find a 'bad guy' in hiding. In the UK, I've worked with several handlers and their dogs whose task it is to find bat carcasses spread over massive areas in order to survey the impact of wind farms on the native bat population. I'm forever excited to think that we're only scratching the surface as far as the potential a dog's nose has to help us detect disease, protect wildlife and save lives.

That said, whenever I drop a treat on the floor, I still

have the audacity to point it out to my dog so he can find it! Like he needs my help. Who am I kidding!!?

With all this in mind, let's turn Pablo into not only a sniffing dog, searching for his toys or food, but go the whole hog and teach him the process of becoming a properly trained Detection Dog. Let's give him the nourishment he deserves. It's so impressive to see a dog who loves his work searching for a designated target scent and although I'm guessing/hoping explosives and narcotics are a tad tricky for you to get your hands on, we can certainly train him to locate and indicate the presence of other target scents, such as birch oil, which you can easily buy online or from a health food shop. You could also use clove or gun oil.

You will need:

- Two clean, empty sample pots, approximately 10ml in size

- A 'target' scent that is safe for dogs and, to avoid any confusion, a scent that is unique to Pablo such as gun oil, clove or birch oil

- A clean, empty jam jar with a well-fitting lid

- A packet of cotton wool balls

- Disposable gloves

- 🐾 Six large Tupperware boxes

- 🐾 Treats

Preparation:

- 🐾 Drill lots of air-holes in the lids of the sample pots and the lids of the Tupperware boxes.

- 🐾 Drip two drops of the target scent onto each cotton wool ball (you only need a handful!) and place them into the sealed jam jar.

- 🐾 For safety, ensure lids are always secure to avoid ingestion.

- 🐾 Wear your treat pouch so it sits behind your back, not in front or on your hip.

STEP ONE: CONDITION THE 'CHOOSIES'

Put a chair in the middle of the room (somewhere it isn't normally placed to paint a unique picture for Pablo). Sit with your two hands behind your back, have the treats in one hand and leave the other hand empty. As Pablo sits or stands in front of you between your knees, say 'Choosies' and pull your two closed fists out in front of you.

Let Pablo sniff and explore each hand and when he settles his focus and sniffs the treat-laden fist, say 'Good!', open your hand and let Pablo enjoy the goodies.

Repeat several times, sometimes with the treats in your left hand, sometimes in your right. Each time he determinedly sniffs the correct hand say, 'Good!', open your hand and treat. What we're doing here is laying the foundations of 'sniff and find' which, when established, we'll transfer over to the 'target' scent later on in a real smarty-pants fashion.

STEP TWO: INTRODUCE THE POTS

Pablo's now twigged that when you sit on your chair in the middle of the room the game of Choosies is about to start...

Repeat the above, but rather than the treats being in your one hand, have the treats in one pot, and the other pot empty. Bring your hands around to the front of you as before and let Pablo explore each pot. When he settles to sniff intently on the winning pot say 'Good!', quickly place the two pots back behind your back and give him a treat from your pouch (remember, to save confusion and distraction, have the treat pouch behind your back). Randomly swap the 'treat pot' between your hands to ensure Pablo isn't just a lucky guesser! When Pablo is consistently settling on the correct pot – the one with the treat in it – we're ready to move to step three...

STEP THREE: THE SEARCH

Place your 'treat-filled pot' into one of the Tupperware boxes (with lots of holes in the Tupperware lid). And place the Tupperware box on the floor. Say to Pablo 'Find it' and when he targets the box with his nose and sniffs at it with enthusiasm, say 'Good!' and for the first few repetitions, you can kneel down with him to open the lid of the box and then the lid of the pot to get him the treats he's been sniffing. It's nice to reinforce in position like this for the first few sessions to keep his focus on the boxes, but after a short while, as long as he's loving the game, you can simply say 'Good!' and reinforce the correct indication with a treat from your pouch. That way you won't have to keep reloading the treat pot each time!

STEP FOUR:
BOX DISCRIMINATION

As above in Step Three, but add an empty 'dummy' Tupperware box a couple of metres away from the Tupperware box on the floor that's got the treat pot in it. Start your search at the empty box and, as with the Choosies game, ignore when he sniffs the dummy box but say 'Good' and reinforce when he targets the treat-pot box. When he's consistent, add a second dummy box, then a third, then a fourth and then a fifth. Keep the treat-pot box in the same position on the floor as it'll be putting down its own little scent-pad, but you can mix the dummy boxes around after each successful repetition to proof the behaviour. For example, have the boxes in a line, two metres between each, and sometimes have two dummy boxes at the front of the line for him to investigate before Pablo hits the motherlode, sometimes three, and so on. Feel free to practise both on- and off-lead.

STEP FIVE: CREATING THE
SCENT LIBRARY

I'd like you to avoid contaminating your training area as much as possible, so away from Pablo and ideally in a room he doesn't go into, such as your bathroom, you can now prepare your kit to start the process of adding the birch oil to Pablo's *scent library*. Pop your disposable gloves on to avoid contaminating your hands with the scent (if you want to be really *CSI*, use tweezers!) and remove one of the birch oil-impregnated cotton wool balls from the jam jar and place it into one of your sample pots. This is now your *target scent pot*. Take your gloves off and head back to your original Choosies chair in the middle of the room as per Step One. As soon as Pablo sees you sat in the chair with your hands behind your back, he'll go, *Lovely stuff, I know what's coming next...*

As before, say 'Choosies' but this time just bring the *target scent pot* around to the front, as soon as Pablo sniffs the pot to explore say 'Good!', remove the pot and give him a treat. After several successful repetitions, start bringing two pots around to the front, the target scent pot and the empty pot. Continue to reinforce Pablo for focusing his sniffing on the target scent pot. That's it, you've now added birch oil to Pablo's scent library.

STEP SIX: THE TARGET SEARCH

All that's left now is for Pablo to not only *indicate* the presence of the birch oil as above, but to also *locate* it. First the Search, then the Find.

The way to do this is to first do a few sessions of the target-scent pot in the Tupperware boxes as per Steps Three and Four, and then to progress to hiding the target scent pot in other locations such as under boxes in the garage, in the garden behind a tree and so on.

That's it! You now have your very own Detection Dog - go get yourself and Pablo a hi-vis jacket, the world's your oyster!

Start the whole process indoors to keep the environmental influence to a minimum, but once you progress to searching outdoors, you'll be fascinated to see how elements such as wind direction can affect the *scent picture*. For example, if the wind is gently blowing left to right and Pablo is searching a row of bags out on the lawn, he may be within one metre to the left of the hide and not indicate, as the wind is blowing the scent away from him; however, he may be five metres to the right of the hide and immediately indicate and home in on the target as the birch oil breeze hooks him in.

My students love it when I ask them to check the wind direction before a search. All Rambo-like, they throw grass into the air and suck a finger. Give it a week or two and they start turning up to class in camouflage trousers, dirt rubbed into their face, knife in their belt, the whole nine yards!

Once you've locked in all the above behaviours with Pablo, you can go back to Step One and start to add a second odour to his scent library, perhaps gun oil, working as before from Step One through to Step Five and beyond.

I think scent detection sessions are going to be perfect physical and mental outlets for Pablo. Indeed, they are a real opportunity for all dogs to really show off their skill set. I love detection work as it soon develops into a real 'team-game', the pair of you 'hunting' as a family and celebrating the Find together.

For any dog, from high-energy go-getters to elderly or physically impaired dogs, scentwork is often the answer.

SETTLE

Hi Steve,

Hope you can help. A couple of months ago, I took in a rescue Dobermann called Disco and all is going great. I love him to bits but I've noticed in the evenings that he seems a little hesitant to actually relax and settle down. His health is spot on and he doesn't need the toilet, I just think (hope!) that he's so happy in his new forever home with me that he's afraid to relax in case I sneak off and leave him! I appreciate this is all new to him as he was rescued from a breeder's kennels, but I want to help him as much as I can.

We've begun training down and stay on a mat, but he seems permanently ready to spring up when released. I've started to introduce little windows of separation between us during the day with the use of child gates, having him in another room and times when I go out shopping and thankfully he seems relaxed enough. I'd just like some advice on how to help him settle with me in the evenings, and maybe some 'settling' tips that I can use when we go on vacation to our caravan.

Many thanks,
Alison

Hi Alison,

Sounds like you and Disco are on the right track, keep up with the short sessions of separation (see page 127) as this will help build Disco's resilience and confidence when away from you. Make sure those moments of separation are paired with pleasant associations for Disco, such as a stuffed food toy.

It's important we distinguish the difference between a 'Down Stay on a Mat', and a 'Settle'. My attitude to 'Settle' as an exercise is that we don't actually *teach* it like a 'Sit' or a 'Down' *per se*, but that we approach it much more holistically. We need to ensure we provide the correct opportunities and outlets throughout the day for sufficient physical and mental release, prior to then providing the correct environment and opportunity for Disco to exhale, relax and voluntarily *rehearse* his settling.

Imagine someone coming to you and saying 'Settle!' Unless they're Derren Brown, it's just not going to happen without all of the other variables being in place for you to genuinely relax. To that end, we're not going to put settle on a verbal cue, we're not going to *ask* for it, we're merely going to set the scene for appropriate rehearsals...

After an honest full day of activity and following his evening meal and subsequent piddle (so Disco doesn't have any ants in his pants), head into your living room and create the kind of set-up that will be repeated in the future: TV on, draw the curtains, dim the lights...

How you hold your body during this exercise is really important and you can pass on some valuable information to Disco that now's the time to chill. It may sound a little whacky, but as you sit and relax on the sofa, let out a few long, drawn-out breaths as you relax your shoulders and sink into the sofa yourself. Dogs, like us, are very sociocentric animals and will pick up on and, importantly, mirror how the rest of the group are feeling.

Don't believe me? Let out a few yawns when you're with your dog. After a while your dog will start yawning also. Depending on the situation, dogs will often use yawning as a way to communicate relaxation, with others in the group reciprocating the gesture with a yawn-reply of their own.

In fact, it's not just dogs that find yawns contagious. When I'm lecturing on canine body language and start to speak about yawning, I'm often met with the vision of gaping mouths like a mother bird returning to the nest. Maybe you're battling a cheeky little yawn yourself right now just reading about it? Go on, treat yourself...

Long, audible deep breaths out during settle sessions are much more likely to be received, understood and reciprocated in this case, rather than just verbally asking your dog to settle. Communication *only* happens when it's in the language of the receiver and that realisation is what makes for great parents, teachers, trainers and owners.

Have a container of treats next to you as you sit on the sofa and place Disco's new comfy bed on the floor by your feet where you'd like him to settle. Being a typically curious Dobermann, I'm sure Disco will look to investigate the novelty of the new bed and when he does, gently drop a treat on two onto the bed for him. Remember, at this stage we're not looking to capture any specific behaviour here, so no need for a 'Good'. We're just setting the scene for Disco to comfortably slot into. Then, with your breathing still nice and relaxed... keep a slow, steady stream of treats being laced onto the bed. Placing the treats by Disco's feet and under his chest will encourage him to eventually lie down on the bed. No need to cue it, he'll lie down when he's ready.

> Tip: Work on your settle a few days after you've started work on your 'Down' training. The many successful repetitions of down trained elsewhere will make the movement of lying down a nice default position.

If Disco slips into 'training' mode and starts to offer alternative behaviours, or begins to stare intensely at you or your hands or face for feedback and instructions, just relax, divert your attention and continue your relaxed breathing and posture. Remember, you're not 'instructing', just creating an *opportunity* and environment for Disco to rehearse relaxation and to settle. If it's proving difficult, keep your sessions short.

Don't turn it into a grind or some war of attrition. Tomorrow's another day and you'll have an opportunity to build another thin layer onto any success you've chalked up today. **Practice doesn't make perfect. Practice makes permanent.** Make sure you're practising and repeating for the desired outcome.

- As soon as Disco relaxes again, feel free to continue with the treat drop.

- If Disco settles on the bed in a sit, deliver the slow and steady flow of treats just to the outside of one of his front feet. This will encourage him to shift his weight onto one hip, which, in turn, will help him eventually fold into a relaxed down, when he's ready.

- When he's relaxed and in a down on the bed, keep the treats steadily coming but slowly reduce the frequency. However, I definitely want you to place a treat on the bed for him when he:

✓ Drops his head
✓ Let's out a nice long sigh
✓ Slowly licks his chops as he relaxes
✓ Lays flat out onto one side.

🐾 If Disco is nice and chilled, every now and then feel free to give him a nice, slow stroke, from his shoulders down to the base of his spine.

Keep initial sessions short, go at Disco's pace and add duration over the following few nights. End each session quietly.

Once Disco is settling voluntarily into his bed in the evenings, you'll have the benefit of transferring the bed, and the positive associations it carries with it, to the caravan to help him settle on his holibobs. Remember, the caravan is a new location, so expect to go back a few steps and that you'll need to remind him it's fine to settle. The important thing is for both of you to see the opportunity to settle in the evening as a reward for a fulfilling day.

NAIL TRIMMING

Hi Steve,

We have an adorable Heinz 57 called Rascal who is thought to be around six years of age. We adopted him three years ago from the RSPCA. I'm not lying when I say he is perfect in every way EXCEPT when it comes to nail trimming time – he hates it, but I'm not sure why? We've tried to go slowly once we saw he was curling his lip and grumbling, but to be honest, even just approaching him with the clippers makes him suspicious and he goes from angel to Tasmanian Devil in seconds. Please help us help him.

Margaret

Hey Margaret,

Go you for living with my favourite breed – a rescue. It's so good that you see this as an opportunity to 'help' Rascal. Anytime a dog feels the need to show aggression, that's exactly what they need: help.

Who knows why Rascal is so afraid of the nail clippers; maybe he had an uncomfortable experience in the past with the clippers catching the quick in his nail; maybe it's not the actual clippers at all, maybe it's having his feet touched; maybe he's had a sore shoulder in the past that was agitated when a previous owner held him, who knows?

What we do know is that his fuse has been shortened to the point that even the sight of the clippers is enough to put him over the threshold. What we need to do is lengthen that fuse to as long as possible, to increase his tolerance and, who knows, maybe even teach him to love a manicure!

Poor old Rascal has learned the warning signs already and by the time you're approaching with the clippers, he's already got his dooks up and is expecting the worst. We're going to wipe the slate clean and paint a brand-new picture for him, one that only predicts good things for him.

I always imagine any problem behaviour as a thick piece of rope. I want to unwind that rope and tease out each individual strand. It's always more effective for me to focus on one individual strand at a time. Once I've cleaned up each individual strand, I can then start weaving them back in together again to make a stronger, more reliable rope.

Our strands here are:

- Trimming location
- Trimming approach
- Being touched
- Trimming equipment.

If you've always tried to trim Rascal's nails in a particular room, then let's not start with one arm behind our backs. I want you to start your training in a brand-new environment, so we're not having to deal with any poisoned clues. If you went to a particular pub and were punched in the face, I'm betting your fuse would be fairly short the next time you stepped into the same boozer! I also want you to invest in a nice new blanket for Rascal. A nice novel colour or texture, one that's only going to come out for nail clipping practice. Let's call it 'Trim-Training'™!

Forget about the actual dastardly deed of nail trimming at the moment. Let's go back a good few steps and start building some optimism well before the clippers enter the picture...

THE SET-UP

Picture the scene: you and Rascal are hanging out in the unadulterated room and you've previously planted the new blanket on the top shelf of the cupboard. Have your laden treat pouch hidden away with the blanket also.

Aaaaaaand ... 'ACTION!'

Step One

'Shall we get the blanket? Ohhh, the blaaaann'ket!' as you slowly but excitedly get the blanket down from the top shelf. Make a real ceremony of it as you lay it on the floor, like you're paving the way for the King of Siam himself to tip-toe over it. Really ham it up. No ... really, REALLY ham it up. Once the blanket is on the floor, generously drop pieces of ham, cheese, any treats that Rascal adores, onto it. We're not looking for Rascal to do any particular behaviour here, we're just going through the ceremony of 'charging up' our wonder blanket. Let Rascal enjoy the treats from the blanket and then quietly but deliberately put the blanket and treats back up on the shelf in the cupboard, and then go about your usual daily business. Repeat this two or three times per day and Rascal's body language will start showing you signs of a very positive conditioned emotional response; tail wagging, relaxed spine and happy expectant eyes as you yet again go through your Oscar-worthy, 'Ohh, the blaaaann'ket!' routine. What we are doing here is lengthening Rascal's fuse. We're building optimism and a positive momentum that will get us over any potential speed bumps in the future.

Step Two

Grab your blanket as before and no doubt happy Rascal won't be far away. Rather than raining treats from above as before, wait or, if need be, encourage Rascal onto the blanket, then start the treat-fest. We want to condition that it's now the behaviour of happily being *on* the blanket that makes the good times roll. Repeat this session several times. If he's comfortable, reinforce a few sits and downs on the blanket, if that's the positions you'd like him to be in for nail trimming in the future, but *do not* introduce the clippers at this point; we've a lot more positive predictability to upload before we get to that point.

Step Three

As before, but now when Rascal is on the blanket, I want you to start naming the body parts before you touch him there, to be followed by a treat each time. This builds predictability and removes suspicion. It also creates a positive association with being touched. Again, lengthening the fuse, baby!

Kneel down with Rascal, say 'Shoulder', touch Rascal's shoulder, followed by a treat.

The treat should only appear *after* the shoulder has been

touched. So 'Shoulder' *predicts* the touch, the touch *predicts* the treat. Don't deliver the cue, the touch and the treat all at the same time or we'll lose effectiveness.

Do this for 'Shoulder' (maybe use your left hand each time for Rascal's right shoulder, and your right hand for Rascal's left shoulder). Do whatever's comfortable but most importantly for building trust, be *consistent*). Once you're well-versed in 'Shoulder' and your lefts and rights(!), then move on to the cues below and remember that it's **cue** *followed by* **touch**, *followed by* **treat**:

'paw' (front feet)
'foot' (back feet)

While you're at it, you might as well 'future-proof' for other interactions such as vet visits and grooming. Let's add:

'teeth'
'tail'
'ears'
'eyes' (go through the motion of giving eye drops, you big thespian you!)

Step Four

Now that we've built optimism with being in the room, being on the blanket and being touched, let's start to introduce some optimism around the clippers. Kneel down next to our expectant Rascal on the blanket, 'click' the clippers once behind your back and then give Rascal a treat.

Put simply, the sound of a 'click' = treat.

What we're doing here is working on the nice thin thread of the clipper's sound. Repeat this session several times over the next couple of days.

Next session, work on the sight of the clippers. Then, the smell of the clippers. Then, start putting the sight and sound of the clippers together prior to giving Rascal the treat.

At this stage, the clippers are going nowhere near Rascal's feet, always keep them front and centre, comfortable to look at but posing no threat to him. Nice, slow deliberate movements. No mystery, no suspicion.

You're actually working through a process here called 'desensitisation', which means we're gradually exposing Rascal to the (previously) scary presence of the clippers and the (previously) scary routine of nail trimming, but at an intensity that means Rascal is *aware* of each element, but not negatively aroused. Also, by pairing the clippers with treats, we've reversed his emotional response to be one of positivity, to feeling good about the presence of clippers.

WEAVING THE ROPE BACK TOGETHER

Now that we've cleaned up each individual strand, we can start putting them back together, one at a time to build our final picture. Get your blanket from the cupboard and let Rascal happily get on it. Kneel down next to Rascal, say 'Paw', touch his paw with your left hand, click the clippers a couple of times at arm's length away from Rascal with your right hand, then treat him with your third hand! (That's why God invented treat pouches, available in the foyer on your way out!)

With Rascal always maintaining a relaxed posture and enjoying the session, gradually place and 'click' the clippers closer to Rascal's paw with each repetition until you're at the point where you can say 'paw', take his paw in your hand, clip a nail, then treat. Use the appropriate cue and repeat this step-by-step process for each of his four feet.

Once all is swimmingly well in your 'training' room, you can happily repeat the process again in the room you actually want to be doing your day-to-day nail trimming and grooming in. Remember to be consistent in your blanket set-up and body parts cueing and also take it in small steps, gradually and slowly.

This process works for lots of situations, not just nail trimming – it's also the way to help any dog struggling with activities such as grooming, vet visits, giving medications, etc. Get your thinking cap on well before you start the actual training and figure out how many thin threads you can filter the process into. The more threads you work on individually, the more robust your rehab will be.

TRACKING

Hi Steve,

My 11-year-old Rottweiler Bruno has always been a fairly quiet dog and comes across to others as the 'sensible' one at the park. I'm aware he's not as agile as he used to be, but we love doing things together, so I'm wondering if there's anything new I can add to his repertoire at all that could re-ignite our love of training and maybe help him come out of his shell a little?

Thanks in advance,
Maria and Bruno

Hi Maria,

Yes! I know EXACTLY the activity for you and Bruno!

Without a doubt, if I have a few hours to spend with one of my older dogs, we're going 'Tracking'! Nothing thrills me more than to see an expert doing what they do best, and all dogs are expert trackers.

So, what exactly is tracking? It's when the dog follows a human's footsteps from point A to point B and was in fact traditionally used to catch criminals or locate missing persons. The question is, as with all dog training, why should they?! The answer here is two-fold:

1. It's an innate behaviour for the dog, linking back to the days of yore when they had to make their own living by following and catching their prey. In essence, it just feels so damn good to do.

2. You, *as always*, are going to make it worth their while!

Dogs 'see' the world through their nose. It always tickles me that when the posh scientists perform their cognitive tests on dogs, the majority of the tests are based on the dog's reaction to *visual* cues. That doesn't even scratch the surface of measuring a dog's intelligence as far as I'm concerned. As Einstein said, 'If we judge a fish by their ability to climb a tree, that fish will grow up thinking they're stupid' (and may never grow up to be a lumberjack).

My advice as a trainer is to 'put the tree underwater' – in other words, as teachers, we need to make changes to the environment to help the learner, and also match the exercise to fit the individual students.

MAKING PERFECT SCENTS

No offence Maria, but you stink (to a dog).

Take this book outside to continue reading...

You outside now? Good.

Stamp your foot.

Jump up and down on the spot a few times.

To a dog, where you've just stamped your foot on the ground *smells* distinctly different to the unadulterated ground either side of your footprint. Your footprint will hold the unique scent of crushed vegetation, little pockets of moisture and vapour released from the broken surface, residual scent from the bottom of your footwear, maybe even a few microscopic insects trapped in the mêlée (R.I.P.). Pick a couple of leaves up from the ground. Smell the first one. Now *crush* and smell the second one. Game changer, eh?

Your dog has an olfactory system up to 100,000 times more capable than yours. Proportionally speaking, the part of Bruno's brain that's dedicated to interpreting scent is 40% larger than yours. Amazingly, a dog can indicate a ½ teaspoon of sugar dissolved in an Olympic-sized swimming pool (although why they would want to do that is another matter). As a comparison, I once called my son on my mobile phone to ask if he knew where my mobile phone was.

Us living creatures are made up of cells. Humans are made up of over 37 trillion of the little scamps. Approximately 50 million cells die on a human body every second. A lot of these cells are skin cells, known as skin 'rafts', which are shed and dropped from the body constantly, like a disgusting epidermal snowstorm. The more you stomp, the more you shed. Couple this cascade of body dandruff with the dead cells from your respiratory and digestive tract, it's a wonder our dogs don't spend all day sneezing like Dumbo at a pepper factory.

THEN there's our sweat. My God, is there no end to our fumes!? Not just any sweat though, that'd be too easy. We actually have two types: stress sweat and cooling sweat. They smell differently. That's how a police dog can chase a suspect into a crowded area and still indicate the 'bad guy', even when he's hiding in plain sight among lots of bystanders. Bad guys smell different. Bad guys smell bad.

Still jumping up and down? Sweet. As you're doing so, those rafts are falling from your body and hitting the ground like glitter from a Christmas tree. The scent will create a 'cone' and lie around where you're stood. If the breeze is right-to-left, the scent-cone will shift to your left; if the breeze is heading towards your right, well, that's where the rafts will head to. The real hotspots of the track will be your footprints, but always bear in mind that those footprints sit within that stinky-monkey-scent-cone your body permanently oozes.

Let's have a look at the stages to work through so you and Bruno can become a Tracking Team:

You're going to need the following kit:

- 🐾 A well-fitting harness with a back attachment for the long line

- 🐾 A long line, approximately five metres in length

- 🐾 A marker pole that you can stick in the ground

- 🐾 Treats

- 🐾 Toy

Ideally, find yourself a nice piece of 'clean' ground that hasn't been walked over by others for a good few hours. The cleaner the ground, the easier it'll be for Bruno to distinguish your footprints. Your first few tracks will be five-to-ten metres or so in length, but you'll soon be needing much more space. If you're the landed gentry and have acres of rolling pastures, good for you; if not, get up early before the rest of the *oi polloi* and head to your local football pitches or park to lay your first few tracks. Ready?

LAYING THE TRACK

1. Without Bruno, walk a few steps forward so you're onto nice undisturbed ground and stick the marker pole into the ground next to your left heel so you know your starting point.

2. At the base of the pole, put a treat in your footprint.

3. With your feet together, shuffle forward, like a kid pretending to be a choo-choo train, and every 30 centimetres or so, place a treat behind your heel onto the track you've laid.

4. With a bit of quick Maths, I reckon you should be placing approximately 15–20 treats over your first track of five metres. Essentially what we're doing here by laying food in your footsteps is saying to Bruno, 'You know that unique smell I introduced you to (of human footprints) at the base of the start pole? It's in your interest to follow it...'

5. When you get to five metres from your start pole, place the toy at the end point where you stand.

6. Turn around and walk back to your start point

along the track you've already laid. It's important you stay on your track as you return past the start pole, so you don't inadvertently lay a second, confusing cross-track.

While you're doing this, if Bruno is the kind of dog to stay chilled and not get too over the top, you can place him in a down or have a friend hold him on-lead. If we were working with a very excitable dog, we'd lay the track out of sight to prevent over-arousal.

COMPLETING THE TRACK

Once the first track is laid, take Bruno with the long line attached to the back of his harness, and introduce him to the treat at the base of the start pole, as you say, 'Seek on'. Hold the line a few inches from where it meets the harness with one hand and, with the other, reach right the way down to the ground to point out where the first treat lies. Remember, this is very new to both of you. Bruno will soon pick up what this tracking game is all about but at this stage he'll have no idea. Your job is to nurse him along the track and to discover the treats along the way, so he can connect the dots to realise that following the unique footprints leads to reinforcement. Also, handle the long line in a way that for the first few repetitions it's nice and short, so you and Bruno stay connected.

Stand sideways onto Bruno so your knees are level with his shoulder as he sniffs along the ground. To avoid your smell fouling the area of the track, try not to get ahead of Bruno. As he goes forward along the track, you can sidestep with him so you're ready to point out the next treat. Nurture him along to follow the trail of treats. Stay nice and slow to allow him to find the treats and, if he seems keen enough to try and find the next one, LEAVE HIM TO IT!

My problem as an enthusiastic youngster was always to try and encourage the dog, no matter what activity, but the fact is if the dog is already tracking, then us saying anything too much in the early stages can only act as a distraction. I remember a wise old trainer saying to me once, 'You can't push a dog with a tracking line', which roughly translates as 'Shut up!' If Bruno stops and looks up, then you can gently point out the next treat to him to get him back on track.

When you get to the end, the toy is there as a visual marker to let you know there's no further track to follow. Be aware that even many of the most toy-crazy dogs will often ignore their toy at this stage because they're in tracking-mode. That's fine, in fact, it's great! It's information that they're digging the new activity you're introducing them to and that they're 'in the zone'.

If they are super-toy-crazy and, after a few repetitions, seem more interested in getting to the end to play rather than enjoying the treats on the track, simply swap out the toy for a more boring marker such as a glove. At this stage, we want the dog to embrace the joy of the journey, rather than the destination.

If Bruno falls into a happy medium where he steadily enjoys the treats along the track and he's happy to find his toy – cool, feel free to have a play when you get to the end to celebrate a job well done.

Over time, increase the length of the track and observe how the wind direction may 'push' Bruno to one particular side of the track as he follows the scent. If this happens, he's not wrong, he's just following where the scent lays heaviest. That's the thing with tracking, the dog will always know best. Once you get into your tracking, it'll really encourage you to look at the world from Bruno's perspective and wonder at the amazing senses and skills that dogs possess.

With the context of the harness and long line, plus being introduced to the base of the start pole and you saying 'Seek on', Bruno will learn that the footprints lead to food. Initially, the scent of the footprint acts as the food bowl but with enough repetition, once the connection has been made, you'll notice that Bruno will start to walk over many of the treats as the sheer joy of tracking will take over. Awesome: you can then start to become more skimpy with your treats. Rather than laying them every footprint you can lay them every three, then every five, then every seven and so on. If he struggles, increase your food drops on the

The Scentwork Kit

'Choosies' for target scent

Scentwork

The Search…

…the Find!

'Settle' down with a good book (ahem!)

Learn to love the clippers

'A clicker is approximately 1/1000000th the size of a double decker bus.'

Laying the track

Seek on...

Following the track…

…LOVING the track!

Retrieves

Extinction Bursts:
We all have 'em!

The Rucksack Walk

The power of choice

Summer

Nancy. Every time!

next track to maintain his confidence and, as always, don't be too greedy too soon with your expectations.

As well as increasing the distance of your tracks, you can also 'age' them. 'Ageing' a track means you'll lay it, then leave it 10 minutes before you introduce Bruno to the start pole. If he's doing well, age the next track longer; if he struggles, reduce the time the track has to settle before running it with Bruno. The older the track, the narrower the corridor of scent will become as the peripheral edges of the scent cool down and dissipate, leaving the stronger source of the track to sit in your footsteps.

As you progress, you can get a friend to lay the tracks for you and, to really ignite Bruno's passion, take him tracking at dawn or dusk when the natural 'tracker-within' is programmed to go hunting. After a few weeks of tracking you'll be able to add more and more distance, start to add a few 45- or 90-degree turns into your track and, if you're anything like I used to be, you'll soon start cancelling appointments just so you can sneak off to do a day's tracking with Bruno!

I'm excited for the pair of you. Tracking rocks and, honestly, it's my favourite activity to do with any of my dogs. Can you tell?!

RETRIEVES

Hello Steve,

I'd like to teach my Fox Terrier, Leno, to play retrieve with me but, at the moment, every time I throw a toy for him he just runs off and 'kills' it?!

Tina

Hi Tina,

A Terrier's gotta Terror!

Certain breeds have been selectively bred over the years to magnify particular aspects of what is called the 'predatory motor pattern':

Eye – Stalk – Chase – Grab Bite – Shake-Kill – Dissect – Eat...

Historically, for a dog to make their own 'living' by catching their energy source in the wild, they'd need all aspects of the predatory motor pattern working like a well-oiled machine so they can locate and catch their prey successfully.

Today, all they'd need is opposable thumbs. However, as we've got that covered for them, they can simply kick-back on the settee flicking playing cards into a top hat while we go out hunting for them.

Anyone that's watched the TV show, *One Man and His Dog*, will have seen how Collies are specialists in the 'Eye-Stalk' phase of easing up onto their 'prey'. For 'Chase' experts, see Greyhounds, Whippets and Lurchers. But when it gets to what part floats a Terrier's boat, it's definitely the 'Shake-Kill' chapter as illustrated by Leno 'killing' his toys when you've attempted your retrieves.

When I used to lecture animal behaviour to students at college, part of the course was to show a video of the

Terrier Man and his team of terriers doing their vermin control duties in an old barn store. It's a difficult watch for a tree-hugging vegetarian such as I, but an important lesson to highlight breed-specific behaviours. The farmers would lift up the bales of hay and out would fly dozens of rats like startled fireworks: *Pow! Pow! Pow!* ... The terriers would follow ... *Pow! Pow! Pow!* As soon as the terrier grabbed the animated rat and shook it until it was dead, passed on / ceased to be / expired and gone to meet his maker, what would the Terrier do? That's right, he would spit the rat out with the immediate intention to go grab and shake another one.

The apex of the game, the peak of the challenge is to grab at the *moving* rat; once the rat stops moving, the Terrier's off to get another fix elsewhere. If you were to put a Labrador in there, then all of the Terrier shake-kill induced carnage of Rattagedon would be going on around them in the barn, yet the Labrador would gently pick up his rat and trot over to the corner... 'I love you, Ratty,' our Labrador would whisper as he stroked his rat. '... I LOVE you. I'm going to NAME you...' he'd say as he lovingly began to knit a little rat-sized baby blue cardigan...

It's the Terrier's selectively bred love of shake-kill that makes that breed the go-to choice for hunting rats. So rather than going against his natural instincts, let's use Leno's pre-loaded software to help us teach the retrieve. As a young apprentice dog trainer working abroad, I was taught, 'If it's in the dog, it'll come out of the dog', so it might as well come out on our terms, to prevent Leno going self-employed!

The below method is particularly potent for dogs such as Terriers that like to shake-kill, but will also be very successful for owners of all breeds as a foundation for building a really strong retrieve...

RATTY RETRIEVES

Kneel on the floor with a rolled-up and knotted tea towel behind your back. When Leno looks to you, say 'GET IT!', pull the towel out in front of you and twitch it along the floor to simulate a little furry creature nipping across the ground. Like a kitten watching a ball of wool, Leno won't be able to resist pouncing and grabbing the towel – let him, we want to bring that Terrierishness to the surface.

Importantly, when Leno grabs the towel, keep your hand nice and low to ensure his feet stay in full contact with the ground; if he's inadvertently lifted up, his bite will become tighter and his neck may become strained, we don't want that. **Keep your movements rhythmic and slow** – a low, sweeping action keeps the game in a sporting judo mentality. Movements that are too rapid and jagged will tip over from judo into a pub fight: too frenzied, angry and competitive, making it difficult to communicate.

With you holding one end of the towel and Leno's mouth

gripping the centre of it (the towel, not your hand!), slowly bring your other hand to hold the opposite end of the towel. When you have a hand on either end of the towel, with Leno's mouth holding the middle, do a few low sweeps of the toy, then 'freeze' your movements – hold your body and the towel dead still, so in essence, the 'rat' is dead.

'Freezing' the movement of the towel with your two hands will 'kill the rat' and allow Leno to loosen his grip; as soon as he lets go, say 'Good!' and give him what the Terrier in him most wants: another chase and grab game of the towel.

Repeat this several times until you're in the position of:

1. 'GET IT!'

2. Leno grabs the towel. *<Slow, low movements as you play together>*

3. You freeze, say 'Out'. *<Leno lets go in anticipation of the next instalment of GET IT!>*

Once the above three stages are reliable, we can then bolt in the **retrieve** element:

1. Say 'GET IT!' as you slide the toy away from you.

2. Leno **runs** and grabs the towel.

3. Leno **runs back to you** for the judo ragging play.

4. You play, then freeze the towel, say 'Out'.
   <Leno, lets go in anticipation of the next instalment of GET IT!>

We now have our very own mini indoor retrieves. Keep practising so Leno learns that *as soon as the toy is in his mouth*, it's in his interest to return it to you asap for the ragging play to commence.

RETRIEVES OUTSIDE

Evolve the indoor Ratty Retrieves above to then take the exercise outside. A common issue here is that when you start throwing the towel further away, there's more chance of Leno becoming distracted by smells or, more likely, keeping the towel all for himself and playing 'stay away'. To combat this, have TWO towel toys (*winks to camera and taps nose, knowingly*).

Throw the first towel and *as soon as Leno picks it up*, produce the second towel in your hand and wave it around like it's the best thing in the world. As far as Leno's concerned, the grass will always be greener on the other side, so he'll be desperate to get the animated towel in your hand. As he runs back to you with the first towel, you can either wait until he drops it or, if you've done your homework as above, say 'Out' and as soon as Towel One hits the ground, say 'GET IT!' and throw Towel Two for him to then chase.

As he chases the second towel, pick up the first one he's retrieved and start waving THAT one when he picks up the one you've just thrown. Every now and then when he returns with the towel in his mouth, encourage him in to you for a game of ragging. That way he'll keep returning nice and close to you so you don't have to do too much mileage to pick up the retrieved towels from the ground – use your brain to save your legs!

For the above method, not only are we playing the cards we're dealt, and therefore tapping into the type of play that Terriers and many other dogs love, we're also borrowing from a method called 'Back Chaining' to get all the components of the retrieve working smoothly together.

WHAT'S BACK CHAINING?

You know when you sing along to a song on the radio, you always nail the first few lines like an absolute Rock God, but then you kinda *la-la-la* fade your way into humming the rest?

> *Hey Jude, don't make it bad, take a sad song, and make it bett-eeer-eeer-er*
> *Remember, to led-der-in-der-der-der, then-you-der-der, la la la la laaa...!*

Learning a song, doing up your laces, retrieving a toy ... they're all what are known as *behaviour chains*. Anytime you describe the full exercise by saying '*... and then ...*' somewhere in the description, you're describing a behaviour chain.

- *Take one lace, pass it under the other lace AND THEN pull both ends tight, AND THEN you make a loop with the lace in your right hand, AND THEN wrap the lace in your left hand...*

- *Throw the toy, AND THEN you ask Leno to run out to the toy, AND THEN he picks up the toy, AND THEN he runs back to you, AND THEN you take the toy...*

The trouble with behaviour chains is that after the first behaviour, the following behaviours tend to be less reliable. The behaviour at the beginning of the chain, behaviour number one, is the behaviour that gets practised the most; behaviour number two less so; behaviour number three even less so, and as for behaviour number four – that's a thin soup, my friend, meagre pickings. Therefore, normally when you first try to learn a behaviour chain, the performance of the behaviours at the start of the chain soon become solid, reliable and set in stone because they're the behaviours you do again and again and again in succession until you hit the trickier, less travelled paths, such as the second line of 'Auld Lang Syne'!

Q: What if we could put the most reliable behaviours at the END of the chain, rather than the beginning? Would the whole behaviour chain become more reliable? (*Answer upside down below for those playing along*)

A: Yes

Welcome to 'Back Chaining'.

How can we use back chaining to teach Leno's Retrieve?
This is the final picture we were aiming at:

1. Say 'GET IT!' as you throw the toy away from you.

2. Leno **runs** and grabs the toy.

3. Leno **runs back to you** for the judo ragging play.

4. You play, then freeze the toy, say 'Out'. <*Leno lets go in anticipation of the next instalment of GET IT!*>

The very first part of the chain we taught, and reinforced (with play), was actually the FINAL step, the part when the toy comes *out* of Leno's mouth. As opposed to trying to teach the behaviour chain starting with Step One, e.g. throw toy, say 'Get It', Leno picks up toy, buggers off over horizon!

We've taught the back end of the chain – Step Four – first, so it becomes familiar and heavily reinforced. Once

Step Four was reliable, we then bolted on the front end of the chain, Steps One to Three.

Retrieves offer an opportunity for you to *engage* with each other, so make sure you don't just turn into a ball-chucking machine. Vary your reinforcers: sometimes have a game of judo with the toy, sometimes swap the toy for a treat and sometimes reinforce a retrieve with the opportunity to do another. To stop too many chases being racked up, which may cause an injury or an adrenalin overload, hold Leno by the harness, throw his toy into the long grass, count five seconds and *then* say 'GET IT'. This will release him into a search for three or four minutes before he bounds out victorious from the long grass, toy in mouth, galloping towards you to celebrate his find with his teammate ... you!

For all of us, it's really valuable to consider the breed of dog we are living with. Traditionally, dogs were forced to adapt to the training plan; today, it's much smarter to adapt our training plan to suit the dog and their individual breed requirements. As my grandad told me, 'If you are going to stroke a donkey, it's wise to stroke them in the same direction as the hair.'

Once you're both well versed in retrieves, change your toys for other articles, and when you're feeling super-cocky, throw your purse into the long grass, count to five, cross your fingers, say 'GET IT', release Leno, and wait...!

THE RUCKSACK WALK

Hey Steve,

I've just moved in with my girlfriend and her Ridgeback, Amber. She is a very sweet dog but in the past has had a few bad experiences with men. We've known each other for some time and although we get on well, when I take her for a walk she seems fairly disinterested in me. I'd really like to invest some time when I move in with her (and my girlfriend!), so we can become good pals and create a friendship that I feel she'd like to make as much as me.

I'm actually a dog handler in the army, so I'm good with the training; it's our relationship I'd like to invest in and I think she'll grow more confident with me if she can make the right choices, rather than being told what to do.

Many thanks,
Dave

Hey Dave,

I've just the thing for you and Amber to help build a bond: the 'Rucksack Walk'!

This idea is perfect for ALL dogs of ALL ages, and will also be pretty damn good for you personally to decompress after your daily manoeuvres!

I always want to give dogs not only what they need but, as much as possible, what they *want*. Living with dogs the way we do, with leads and harnesses, roads and rules, it's hard to see what, given the choice, a dog *would* genuinely choose to do with their time?

I'm lucky enough to have travelled the world talking about dog training and on one particular trip, I found myself following the 'street' dogs of Peru to discover just what dogs love to do when they go 'self-employed'.

The dogs I followed there weren't exactly *street* dogs, they actually lived in homes with their owners, but first thing in the morning the front doors would open and out would come the dogs to hang with their other doggy mates for the day, do what they want, go where they please. Come 11pm, you'd see the doors open for the dogs to return home for their 'bed and breakfast', and then the next day they'd do the same ... and the next, and the next. Not a bad life, to be honest. In fact, it's the way I lived when I was aged 14!

I had an opportunity to find out what dogs choose to do to *enrich* their lives, and here's what I discovered as I

filmed them hanging out in the Plaza De Armas, a large pedestrian square and gardens in the city of Cuzco:

- **They loved to be next to people.**
  Just to *be* with people had obvious value to them.

- **They rarely felt the need to run or chase.**
  By not being restricted to 'a quick walk around the block', they took their time. They would stop to watch the world go by. No panic. No desperation to get from A to B.

- **They didn't bark.**
  No frequent occurrences of arousal or conflict.

- **They were curious.**
  If there was a bag or pocket to investigate, too right they'd investigate!

- **They liked being touched.**
  Long gentle strokes, shoulder to hip, seemed to fit the mood perfectly.

- **They liked to sniff.**
  Novel items in the environment were investigated with a nosy sniff.

- **They liked food.**
  A sneaky treat from a stranger was always welcomed.

These dogs were happy, relaxed, content. These dogs were telling me what dogs choose to do, given the choice.

As I sat there, I wondered, *How can I offer the same choice to our dogs 'back home', without wrapping it up in a bundle of adrenalin?* That's when I came up with the 'Rucksack Walk'.

This is an activity you can do with Amber that will help build trust without pressure, help you spend time together to increase your bond and that will enrich both of your lives; all for only 15 minutes per day. It's a good deal!

I figure that if you and Amber can learn to love hanging out with each other, that's a hell of a start for the rest of your lives as a family.

The Kit

- 🐾 A rucksack
- 🐾 A long line, approximately five metres long (not an extendable lead)
- 🐾 A dog chew
- 🐾 Novelty food in a Tupperware box
- 🐾 A novelty 'Thing', e.g. a comb, a book, a spoon, anything!
- 🐾 Novelty 'smell' in a Tupperware, box e.g. a teabag, an old sock, a catnip toy

🐾 A loaded treat pouch.

The Rucksack Rules

🐾 Don't see this as a 'training' exercise. It's simply a chance to create relaxed bonding time.

🐾 Every word you say is to be a whisper.

🐾 Treat everything that you pull from the rucksack as if it's a precious and delicate baby bird.

🐾 Commit to one 15-minute session per day.

Ready?

THE MOOCH

Drive to your location, park up in a nice quiet spot, clip your loaded treat pouch onto your belt, gently put a long line onto Amber's harness and unload her from the car. A normal length lead here will create too much tension. Use the long line to enable plenty of slack for Amber to wander, without you having to pull against each other.

So many owners start their dog walks like they're launching a missile, then wonder why their dogs are so wound up! Engage your inner Peruvian ...

With the long line connecting you and Amber, I want you to 'mooch' to your destination, which only needs to be a short distance away. The shorter the distance, the less chance of bumping into a distraction or potential revver-upper such as another dog or cyclist.

To 'mooch' means to head in the general direction of your location with Amber, but if she needs to stop to sniff, cool, no rush, let her. If she wants to wander left or right again, no rush, go with her. The only time I want you to stop is if you get to the end of the long line and it goes tight, or if she begins to run. If you do need to stop, wait until the line goes slack, then off you go again to continue your mooch.

If, at any time during your mooch, Amber glances towards you, then capture that behaviour by saying 'Good', then toss a treat to the other side of you, away from her, so she can trot over and get her reinforcement for her connection to you.

The reason I want you to throw the treat out to the other side of you is so she can get reinforced for checking-in with you *and* get another opportunity to sniff and check out the environment. If, at this early stage in the walk, when a dog needs to acclimatise to the environment, the treat came from your hand only, then it becomes a conflict of 'either/or'. They can *either* check out the environment in order to bed-in, relax and feel safe *or* they can come in to you for the treat. By tossing the treat to the side, Amber can get both, it's a win/win, with the result being she can settle into the walk quicker, and trust that you're not going to try and slow down that process.

RECALL CIRCUITS

When you arrive at your location – let's imagine it's by a large oak tree – I want you to visualise a small triangle on the ground, with the three points of the triangle about five metres from each other. Here's where you're going to do a few 'Recall Circuits' to confirm to Amber you're worth hanging out with!

1. Stand next to Amber, say 'Come', place two or three treats by your feet and, as Amber eats, run to the next point of the triangle and face Amber...

2. As soon as she finishes the treats and *lifts her head*, say 'Come', and place a further two to three treats by your feet; again, as soon as she sets off to run towards the treats, you run to the third point of the triangle...

3. Continue to 'rinse and repeat' as many times as you fancy (if either of you have to stop to breathe into a brown paper bag, you've *possibly* done too many circuits).

Once you've blown out any excess energy with your recalls, it's time to settle down into the rucksack elements.

THE MAGIC OF THE RUCKSACK

I don't know about you, but I loved it when our school-teacher used to say, 'You've been so good this week, we can have our story outside today.'

'OUTSIDE?!'

So, to take a leaf out of the teacher's book, let's get away from our formal *classroom* as much as possible with this one. There's no right or wrong, Amber getting nice things isn't going to be contingent on her doing the *right* behaviours for a change. There'll be plenty of opportunities for that during her more formal training, which needs to be built upon the foundations of trust and safety. We're laying those foundations now.

So, sit down on the ground with Amber and, like a sequinned Las Vegas magician, slowly and carefully, but with an engaging flourish, take the rucksack off your back (remember, it's packed full of 'baby birds').

It's this exciting air of anticipation that will hook Amber's attention onto the whole ceremony. Engagement with our dogs doesn't have to condemn all owners to desperately try to be the loudest and most animated thing down the park, that's impossible (and desperately heart-breaking the day you realise you're not even more interesting than fox-poo!). No, it's not the loudest scenes in the movies that get us on the edge of our seat, glued to the TV with 100% undivided focus; it's the suspense, the anticipation and the quiet, intense, whispering scenes as the plot ... is ... finally ... revealed.

That's what we're doing here, so with slow movements and a whispering 'Oh, my word...' soundtrack, slowly unzip the rucksack as Amber curiously watches you, delicately dipping into the bag and, like an apprentice bomb disposal officer, taking the first precious item from the rucksack...

The Novel Scent Box

Slowly bring the box from the rucksack and with a whispering, 'Oh, my, what is it, Amber?', shield it gently in your hands and offer it for Amber to investigate, just a little at a time, like when you catch a frog as a kid and offer to show your mate. As the seconds tick past, slowly open the edge of the Tupperware box a little more each time, let Amber sniff, then gently move the box away. Not too much too soon: offer it again, see if you can get two minutes undivided attention from Amber, a two-minute conversation between the pair of you, just by introducing the scent. I bet you can.

When done, carefully and deliberately place the box back into the bag.

Now it's time for the next box to come from the magician's bag...

The Novel 'Thing'

The 'Thing' can be anything, as long as it's safe for you and Amber to investigate it together. Let's say it's a hair comb. (Which, to be honest, for me, would be a novelty!) As you produce the comb, we want Amber to be saying to herself, OMG, *what's coming next? Seriously, what is it...?* Just like with the novelty smell, the dogs of Peru also loved to investigate novel items, so how can we work to keep Amber engaged and curious about the comb?

- Slowly remove the comb from the rucksack with a whispering commentary and make sure YOU show an intense curiosity of 'What *is* this?' – it will certainly help.

- Hold the comb like a baby bird as you let her poke her nose in to check it out.

- Hold your face down low to the comb and, as Amber nuzzles closer, gently run your finger along the teeth (the comb's, not Amber's), to make that odd *duggaduggaduggadugga* sound, like tumbling dominoes.

- Slowly lift the comb to your mouth and blow through the teeth. (I'm not even going to attempt to write that sound!)

Great dog trainers are creative, here's your chance to shine, Dave! Can you get a couple of minutes of attention out of Amber with the comb? Definitely. Next up, the big one ... FOOD!

The Novelty Food Box

You really shouldn't have to work too hard here to maintain a connection between the two of you, but as food is so precious and special to dogs, make sure you rinse out every drop of potential anticipation and connection before the final payoff.

As trainers and owners, we can sometimes become so obsessed with what *we* want – the behaviours – that we lose sight of what the dog really values: *the food*.

Here's a chance to redress that balance and, rather than swapping five minutes of training for one second of eating, we're really going to double down and enjoy the ceremony of the food...

Like the earlier escapees from the rucksack, bring out the food Tupperware box super slowly like a dog-training Gollum revealing the golden ring for the first time. Ease open the corner of the lid, let Amber get a nose-full first, then slowly take the treat out. Maybe it's half a sausage left over from last night's dinner, perhaps you could break it into 10 small pieces and give her one piece at a time, let her really savour every last morsel.

When it's all gone, place the box back into the rucksack and bring out the chew....

The Chew

The final reveal from the rucksack is the 'Chew'. Chewing helps dogs relax and release all of those feel-good and bonding hormones, so as Ambers chews, let her lie right next to you to keep yourself in that feel-good picture. Remember our relaxing dogs in Peru? Long slow strokes, shoulder to hip.

Once done – no rush – and only when you're ready, pack away the chew, pick up your rucksack and start heading back to your car.

HEADING BACK HOME

As you mooch back to your car, stick to the same rules of only stopping if the long line goes tight or if Amber starts to run. However, this time, if she glances towards you, say

'Good', but now give her the treat directly from your hand by the side of your thigh, as opposed to throwing out across your body away from her.

You've been in the environment together for at least 15 minutes, so there's no longer a need for her to familiarise herself with the place, therefore there'll be no conflict for her to now come in close to you and, let's be honest, you've just invested the last quarter of an hour to prove you actually *are* the most interesting thing in the park, what with your curious presentation skills and your bag of tricks!

Don't tell anyone, but the treats you gave on your mooch out were actually reinforcing Amber's eye contact and recalls, and the treats given from your hand on the way back, they're an investment for future loose lead walking.

Every day's a school day, eh?

Once back in the car you can head home knowing you've given Amber the enrichment that, given the choice, she'd choose for herself. And you know what? After a few days, I bet *you* start feeling better about your walks together also.

Not only are rucksack walks great for building a relationship, but they are also the perfect activity to offer puppies, older dogs, injured dogs, dogs with anxiety, adrenalin addicts, dogs in rescue ... in fact, EVERY SINGLE DOG.

Come to think of it, as you're a military dog handler, I'm sure there's a healthy benefit for dog AND handler to do a rucksack walk at the end of a shift to help both parties 'come down' and decompress after what could be quite a stressful patrol.

There you go – the rucksack walk. What a return for an investment of only 15 minutes per day to help Amber feel loved, safe and optimistic about her future family life with you.

PART 4
LEARNING ABOUT DOGS, LEARNING ABOUT TRAINING

This section is the webbing that pulls everything together. We'll look not only at what and how to train our dogs, but we'll also drill down into the many training tools at our disposal. We'll discuss training classes, creative ways to get more of the behaviours we love from our dogs, plus the many factors to take into consideration as our dogs hit the important ageing milestones.

LIFE REWARDS

Hi Steve,

Every day my Border Collie Marge and I are learning together and thanks to Easy Peasy Puppy Squeezy I think I've got the 'training bug', so watch yourself, when I leave school I'm after your job! Sometimes when when we are out, I worry I may be missing training opportunities as I don't always have my treats or toys with me. Is there anything else I can do?

Callum

Hi Callum,

Ha! Good for you, brother, let me know when you're ready to take over the reins!

That's a great question. Too many people think that 'training' only happens 8pm to 9pm at the village hall on a Thursday evening. In my book, that's potentially 167 hours of missed opportunities per week. (Don't bother checking, I've got a calculator on my watch!)

The good news is you can definitely reinforce the behaviours you want more of, even if you're not kitted out in your 'training' gear.

What we're going to use here is 'Life Rewards'.

When we're with our dogs, we're surrounded by potential activities our dogs love to do such as being let off the lead to 'go play', jumping into the car to visit the park or entering the vet's waiting room to get a treat and a cuddle from the vet nurse. The skill of using life rewards is to firstly recognise which activities your dog loves to do, and to then give access to those activities *in exchange for the behaviours from your dog that you love.*

Try the exercise below to expand your reinforcement toolkit and to help Marge understand that it's in her interest to do the right behaviour all the time, not just at class:

Make a list of 20 things Marge loves to do. If she loves it, jot it down. For example, with Asbo, my first Malinois, my list would look like this:

Ear scratches

Biting tyres

Digging holes

Biting the hose pipe

Catching water from the hose pipe

Retrieving white plastic garden furniture (don't tell my wife!)

Searching for drugs

Getting in the van

Getting out of the van

Chasing me

Being chased by me

Playing with other dogs

Biting 'bad' guys

Catching treats

Belly rubs

Chasing a ball

Having his ears rubbed

Having his butt scratched

Getting on my lap

Going into the vets

If I wanted to improve, let's say, Asbo's 'Sit with Duration', I'd then ask myself (assuming I was in the right environment): *Could I use any of the above activities to reinforce that behaviour?*

Catching treats? Sure! I'd ask for a sit, count five seconds and, if he's still in the sit, I'd say 'Good' and toss him a treat to catch.

Belly rubs? 100%. I could ask for a sit, step away a couple of steps, count up to 10 seconds and if he remained in position I'd return to him, say 'Good' and give him a good belly rub.

Let's put it another way: is there any activity listed above that I couldn't use to reinforce an appropriate behaviour from Asbo? Absolutely not. If it was available and Asbo loved it, too right I'd use it to reinforce the right behaviours. That way we were both happy, I'd get what I wanted, and so would Asbo. Obviously if your dog loves swimming in the sea but you live in Birmingham, then that might be tricky, but you get my drift!

Certain life rewards will be obvious to the dog, so there's no need to 'name' them. For example, you get to the door of the Doggy Daycare premises where Marge loves to go in and play. As you get to the door, you don't want Marge to barge in, so you stop. Marge is facing the door, she knows exactly the good times that lie ahead. Ask her to sit and when she does, say 'Good!' and in you go. You've got the behaviour you want (sit), you've 'marked' the behaviour

('Good!') and the behaviour has been reinforced (going through the door). With repetition, not only will Marge be sitting at the door before you've even asked her to (she is a Collie, after all!), but she'll LOVE doing her sit for you, because it leads to AWESOMENESS!

I'll give you another example with Asbo. Unfortunately, he died young so I always look back to him with rose-tinted glasses; however, he *was* the best dog in the world ... Asbo was perfect. It seemed I only had to think about asking him to do something and there he was, all expectant eyes and ready for action. Perfect. Then one day, he hit adolescence – see page 242!

We were walking towards one of our training fields. 'Come!' I shouted to Asbo as he jogged away from me. 'Nope!' he said back over his shoulder as he stuck up two fingers and carried on jogging to dig his favourite rabbit hole!

Oh no! any normal person would say.

Hurrah, a training opportunity, said moi!

I got to work. Here's what I did:

1. With Asbo on the lead, we'd stand a couple of metres from his favourite rabbit hole. As soon as I released him, it was obvious what he was going to do ... 'Go dig!' I'd say, then release him to go dig. We'd repeat several times.

2. Then we'd stand, on-lead, a couple of metres from the hole and wait ... only when Asbo <u>glanced up to me</u> would I say, 'Go dig!', and then off he'd go, digging to his heart's content...

   I'd then ask him to sit a couple of metres from the hole. I'd have a long line attached to his harness and I'd walk few steps behind him. He'd be two metres from the hole and looking at his quarry, I'd be five metres away. Only when he had made a concerted effort to look over his shoulder and <u>give me eye contact</u>, would I say, 'Go dig!', and off he'd go.

3. Next stage, with Asbo in a sit as before, I'd reel the slack long line out between us. When he looked away from the hole to me I'd say 'Come!', then <u>when he ran to me</u> to be touched I'd then say, 'Go dig!', and back he'd go to the hole for what he most enjoyed.

We evolved the training to work off-lead, and eventually the result was that Asbo LOVED it when I shouted 'Come!', as he had learned that the behaviour it cued – the recall – led to *the best stuff in the world*, which at that time, at that place was ... digging! We were both happy, which is all I ever wanted for me and Asbo. I still miss him.

Being aware of, and using, life rewards is not only a great

way to maintain previously introduced behaviours, but will keep you tuned in to always looking out for reinforcement opportunities and, therefore, **training opportunities**.

So, there you go, Callum, you and Marge are surrounded by wonderful reinforcement opportunities all of the time and, as the old dog training saying goes, whenever the two of you are together, one of you is training the other one! I hope you and Marge have as much joy training together as myself and Asbo did. It's dogs like these that give us the training bug, so stay on track, keep looking at the world through Marge's eyes and when you're ready to continue your vocation, hit me up!

CLICKER TRAINING

Hi Steve,

I keep seeing the term 'Clicker Training' and 'Shaping' when reading about dog training but I don't really know what it means. Can you shed some light on those phrases for me please?

Thank you!
Ciara

Hi Ciara,

When training, we know we want to reinforce the dog for doing the behaviours we want more of. That's why smart recalls are sometimes followed with the throw of a tennis ball, or nice loose lead walking is often met with a treat or two. We know what we're reinforcing. But how does the dog know?

Imagine if you were walking around the supermarket and suddenly a funny little store manager comes running down the aisle towards you, hands you a £5 note, then runs off again. Weirdo! You continue your browsing and a few minutes later, here he comes again ... sprinting along the aisle, gives you another fiver and off he disappears. Now, you don't know what's happening here, you don't know why this fella's handing out cash like your favourite bachelor uncle at Christmas, but you like it!

Here's the deal: as you mosey around the supermarket, the store manager is up in his office watching the CCTV. He's desperately trying to teach you to touch the products on the top shelf. He's read ALL the books on training and behaviour, so he knows by now that to make a behaviour more likely to reoccur, he needs to reinforce the 'student' for doing the desired behaviour.

THERE! He's just spotted you touch another product on a top shelf. Off he jumps from his chair, runs down the stairs, enters the shop floor and zooms past the 'Condiments and Sauces' to grease your palm with yet another 'Lady Godiva'. He knows what behaviour he's reinforcing, but the problem is, as yet, *you don't.*

Let's be honest, if you knew what specific behaviour was earning you these £5 notes, I bet you'd do that behaviour a lot more frequently!

How can we help the store manager communicate the specific behaviour he wants you to do more of?

Take Two: the store manager is watching you on the CCTV as you saunter along the tinned goods aisle. You pick up a tin of peaches from the middle shelf, read the label, put it back. You then reach up to the top shelf and the second your hand touches the baked beans ... 'DING!', the store manage rings a bell that chimes out on the store's PA system, he runs down the aisle and pops a lovely crisp £5 note into your hand. On you go, suspiciously wondering how you can earn yourself another fiver ... you pick up an orange from the display in front of you and put it into your trolley. Then a bag of potatoes from the floor. Nothing. You then reach up to a packet of pumpkin seeds on the top shelf and the second you do, 'DING!', there's the sound of the bell, followed moments later by the store manager who hurries towards you and places a fiver into your now expectant outreached hand. You know when he's running towards you that it predicts another deposit into your now bulging purse, but how can you get him to run to you in the first place?

You turn a corner to face the layers of display shelves in front of you. You put your arm out and investigate the goods, when your arm eventually reaches up and grabs the box of tissues on the top shelf 'DING!', down he runs and gives you MORE money!

Ah ha! you think to yourself, *I've cracked it! It's when the bell rings that he then gives me money! How can I make him ring the bell again?*

You continue your shop, picking up the crisps from the middle shelf ... nothing. You hopefully take a loaf of bread from the bottom shelf but you're disappointed to hear no bell. You keep trying ... then you stop at the nuts and reach up to take a packet of cashews from the top shelf and, as you do, 'DING! CASHBACK! *It's when I touch a product on a TOP SHELF! That's what makes the bell ring that makes the store manager appear in the aisle to give me the cash.*

By your powers of deduction, and by the store manager using a 'marker' – in this case a bell – to 'mark' the exact time you did the desired behaviour, you've figured out what behaviour to do again, and again, and again, to earn you lots of lovely dosh!

That's the power of 'marking' a behaviour *prior* to giving the reinforcer.

Instead of a 'ding' over the supermarket tannoy, in dog train-ing, a 'clicker' is often used to 'mark' the desired behaviour. A clicker is simply a little box that is approximately 1/1000000th the size of a double-decker bus that when pressed with your thumb makes, unsurprisingly, a *click* sound. A clicker isn't an essential tool to mark behaviours though, what's important is that the behaviour is marked.

Sea mammal trainers may use a whistle, dog trainers may use a clicker or they may just say 'Good' or 'Yes'. Trainers of deaf animals may use a flashing light or a hand signal. Some people find the use of a clicker too awkward; that's fine, as long as the behaviour is marked correctly and consistently. If you wish to use only verbal markers, that's also fine, just stick to a marker word of one syllable and you'll be fine.

Certain owners used to get flustered at my classes and say, 'Oh, I can't deal with having to use a clicker ON TOP OF holding the lead and having to worry about my treat pouch!' I'd be like, 'But man, you DROVE here!'

It doesn't matter what it *is*, but it does matter what it *means*.

For the majority of my answers in this book, I suggest the use of the word 'Good' to mark the desired behaviour prior to reinforcement. Just the click or 'Good' is not enough though, it needs to be paired with something the dog loves (the reinforcer) in order for the dog to learn that the behaviour they just did pays well, so is worth repeating!

TIMING

Using a marker is like clicking a camera and taking a photograph of the dog the second they do the desired behaviour. You then effectively show the dog the photo and say, 'See what you're doing there in that pic? *That's* why you got the treat.' The dog then learns what behaviour pays the dividend. Dogs, like us, repeat the behaviours that pay well. **What gets treated gets repeated.**

SHAPING

Right, get ready for some science-talk...

Shaping, is when the trainer (you!), reinforces the dog for performing any incremental step towards a final, target behaviour. A nice simple example is the 'hot and cold game' you used to play as a kid. Remember? Your friend would go out of the room and your job was to decide on a 'final, target behaviour' you were going to try and get your partner to do, simply by you saying 'hot' or 'cold'.

Let's say the final target behaviour was to 'touch the fridge'. They'd come into the room and start looking around. When their eyes looked towards the corner of the room with the fridge in it, you'd say 'Hot!' They'd take one step in the direction of the fridge, you'd say 'Hot'. Again, they'd head towards the fridge area, 'Hot!' Then perhaps they'd take a step in the wrong direction (the fool!), away from the fridge. 'Cold' you'd say (normally in a deeper voice, I don't know why?). Back they'd go towards where they last got their positive feedback, 'Hot' you say. They're getting closer, hardly any 'Colds' and plenty of 'Hots' until they're within touching distance of the fridge. 'HOT!' you'd shout ... you can't take the excitement ... 'Boiling hot! Boiling hot!' until you finally SHAPE them to do the *final target behaviour* – touching the fridge.

Well, shaping in dog training is similar to that. Only you're not using 'Cold' at all, and instead of 'Hot' you're using a 'Click' or 'Good' followed by a treat.

Let's say you wanted to teach your dog to close the door with their paw. The several shaping stages may look similar to below:

Put a sticky Post-it note on the floor.

- Dog looks at Post-it note, click and treat
  (Instead of 'click and treat', let's use C&T.
  I'm paid by the hour here, not the word count!)

- Dog steps towards Post-it note, C&T

- Dog gets within a metre of Post-it note, C&T

- Dog sniffs Post-it note, C&T

- Dog touches Post-it note with their foot, C&T

Note: Each time you C&T, drop the treat near you; that way the dog can go back and offer the behaviour again from a clean starting point.

Once the dog is comfortably and consistently going back and touching the Post-it note with their foot after each C&T, then we can start changing the picture...

- Put Post-it note by the edge of the room, on the floor next to the closed door

- Dog touches Post-it note with their foot, C&T

- Repeat until fluid

- Put Post-it note so it lies 75% on the floor, but 25% curled up against door

- Dog touches Post-it note with their foot, C&T

- Repeat until fluid

- Put Post-it note so it lies 50% on the floor, 50% curled up against the door

- Dog touches Post-it note with their foot, C&T

- Repeat until fluid

- Put Post-it note so it lies 25% on the floor, 75% curled up against door

- Dog touches Post-it note with their foot, C&T

- Repeat until fluid

- Put Post-it note so it's 100% stuck vertical against the bottom of the door

- Dog touches Post-it note with their foot, C&T

- Repeat until fluid

Next stage...
Gradually increase the height of the Post-it note on the door so it's at a comfortable height for the dog to 'paw' at.

Next stage...
Have the door ever-so-slightly open, just balancing on the latch so the slightest touch from the dog on the door closes the door, resulting in you C'ing & T'ing!

Next stage...
Gradually have the door more open inch by inch for each repetition, with the dog successfully closing the door each time to earn the C&T.

Next stages...
Cut the Post-it note in half so it's less of a target. Leave the open door as the prominent target...
Cut the Post-it note in half again, so it's now a quarter the original size; again, the main clue is the open door...

Remove the Post-it note completely, continue to C&T each time the door is 'pawed' shut.

We're now in a position where, given the chance, the dog will head over to the door at any opportunity during the 'shaping' session to close it and earn a prize. Your dog now knows HOW to do the behaviour.

Next, we need to look at adding a cue so your dog will know WHEN to do the behaviour. If we don't add a cue, then the dog will forever be running around the house slamming doors like a skint dad stressing about the heating bills!

Adding the Verbal Cue

- Set up your session as before. Then, *the second the dog actually closes the door* say 'DOOR!' to coincide with the behaviour occurring, C&T (repeat several times).

- After C&T'ing the previous repetition, say 'DOOR!' a split second prior to the behaviour occurring; when it does occur, C&T (repeat several times).

- Say 'DOOR!', dog heads over to the door, closes it, you C&T.

You've now 'named' the behaviour, you can cue it to happen when you say 'Door', and you only reinforce it happening *if* you've given the cue.

Make sure the behaviour is nice and reliable before you add the cue. The rule for adding cues is: **don't name it till you love it!**

So, there you go, hope that helps. Click!

ADOLESCENCE

Hi Steve,

Help! My 10-month-old Bernese Mountain Dog Dave has changed overnight from being the sociable fur-ball of a puppy who loved everyone and everything, into a dog that seems to be either over-excited by everything or intolerant of everything. He's basically determined to give me a tough time at any given opportunity! I've no doubt he's trying to test my limits and has even started standing still on walks if he doesn't fancy going any further. He's a big dog, so carrying him is not an option! Whereas up to a month or so ago he got on with all of the other dogs he met on his walks, he now gets 'picked on' by some dogs and recently he's actually started to be quite aggressive towards other male dogs in anticipation of aggression towards him. His obedience has hit a brick wall. I've started to increase his daily exercise to try and drain some of his excess energy and maybe put him on a more even keel but any other advice will be greatly appreciated.

Martin Pwei

Hiya,

Dig in Martin, it's gonna be a bumpy ride! Welcome to the world of canine adolescence. Rubbish, ain't it? But don't worry, it won't last forever and, believe me, this is the time when Dave *needs you the most*. Contrary to what you think, he's not giving you a tough time: he's *having* a tough time.

Dogs enter into adolescence, depending on breed, between approximately six to 18 months, with the larger breeds arriving a little late to the party but being one of the last to leave. Bernese Mountain Dogs certainly qualify as a large breed, so I'm guessing you're bang in the eye of the storm right now.

During adolescence, all sorts of hormonal fluctuations are at play that affect development such as growth and sexual maturity, as well as an increase in more evolutionary-type behaviours such as a desperation to roam, to explore new territories and to check out the local talent. That drive to wander and explore is fuelled by an increased immunity to risk-taking and, to be fair, from a species developmental point of view, it makes perfect sense for a dog when they hit sexual maturity to want to move away from the 'family' unit to explore and potentially mate – it increases the gene pool and limits inbreeding.

Look at human teenagers for a comparison, the amount of craziness we got up to in our teenage years that we'd never dream of doing now is testament to that. It's how we find our limits and how we can fast-forward our experiences to prepare us for adulthood. Sadly, adolescents often push that risk-taking too far, for example, look at the disproportionate stats for teenage road traffic accidents. Mentally it's also a really tough terrain to negotiate, 75% of behavioural and psychological disorders start during the adolescence phase for humans worldwide.

The spiralling chemicals, such as dopamine and testosterone, that are surging out of Dave like some punk geyser all play a vitally important role in his development, but they also contribute to some iffy temporary traits such as mood fluctuations, impulsivity and a low tolerance to stressors – which make living with him, just for the time being, a little more tricky than usual.

Empathy check: remember what *you* were like as a teenager? I'm betting a bit of a door-slamming, moody, erratic, fly-off-the-handle-at-any-opportunity, dangly armed loon? No offence. As a human, at least we get 13-odd years to prepare for the incoming adolescence storm. Dogs only get a measly six months! Count yourself lucky that Dave doesn't lock his bedroom door, turn off all the lights and play his Stormzy tracks too loud over and over and over again.

At this juncture, it's easy to guess correctly that the most common age bracket for people to dump their dogs into shelters is at ... that's right, six to 18 months. Sometimes I'm left thinking that if people won't love them at their worst, they don't deserve to love them at their best.

At the present time, Dave is experiencing a massive surge in testosterone, in fact, he is producing a lot more testosterone at this age than a fully mature, adult male dog. The increase in testosterone means that other male dogs can sniff him a mile off and are not going to be as forgiving of his presence as they were a few months ago when he still had his 'puppy-licence'.

You mentioned that he has been 'picked on' by other dogs and I'd wager that with a history of those bad experiences, paired with his teenage sensitivity, he's now getting his retaliation in first by being more proactively assertive when he meets other dogs. It's really important that he doesn't carry on practising those aggressive behaviours as it will become the 'norm' for him.

While you're nurturing Dave through adolescence, I really want you to keep his social calendar full of dogs you know he's good with, but please avoid any potential confrontation with unknown dogs or ones he's had recent bad experiences with. It's just while you weather the teenage storm, it's not forever, but 'practice makes permanent' and we want this to be a temporary blip, not a permanent way of life.

The 'over-excited by everything or intolerable of everything' is another interesting canine and human teenage trait – feast or famine, rarely anything in between! Again, the CAPS LOCK intense emotional response explains phenomena such as Beatlemania or why millions of teenagers, and one adult man in his forties, wept for days when One Direction split up. (Even now, as I write, a single tear rolls down my cheek. Don't.)

One thing I really want to address is Dave standing still on walks and refusing to go forward. The smart money says he's not trying to 'test your limits' as you suspect, but rather there's a good chance he's in pain. During adolescence Dave will be going through immense growth spurts (remember our dangly armed teenager?), and those spurts can certainly cause issues such as *panosteitis*, more commonly referred to as growing pains, especially in a rapidly growing large breed such as a Bernese Mountain Dog. His stopping on walks is more likely linked to pain rather than stubbornness. If in any doubt, have a word with your vet.

What we really don't want to do is associate going for a walk with pain; that's a sure-fire way to shorten his fuse and increase his reaction tenfold if he crosses paths with his canine nemesis. We know it's bad enough when someone cuts us up in traffic, but if they cut us up in traffic AND we've got a toothache? Well, let me tell you, someone's gonna get seriously raged upon. Or beeped, minimum.

To that end, increasing his daily exercise to 'drain his energy' might not be the best plan of action. Instead, let him use his nose more to give him some extra mental 'release'. I recommend scatter-feeding him in the garden for his morning and evening meals.

Simply open the back door and throw out his food for him to have a bit of a sniffari. Let him spend a good 30 minutes mooching, sniffing and finding his food for a nice, low-impact mental release session rather than scoffing his food from a bowl in 30 seconds then having the rest of the day to do the devil's work! (In addition, have a good look at the scentwork and tracking chapters for some more constructive nose work ideas).

Now, what else can we do to help you and Dave negotiate the storm together, as a team? Regarding training, you mentioned his 'obedience has hit a brick wall' – of course it has, so did mine when I discovered girls! Swallow your pride and work with the dog in front of you, don't lament for the biddable puppy of yesterday's that baby has flown the nest so you're on to the next, super-important phase of helping Dave become the most optimistic, stable and happy dog he can be. The important thing here isn't actually that today's performance is always better than yesterday's, but that *you're* skilled and pragmatic enough to set your criteria at a suitably achievable level each day. So what if he doesn't spin on a dime and do a down from 50 yards – what is important is that you keep his love of training alive. Far better to get success and heavily reinforce 10 times out of 10 than to keep reaching for a difficult standard and fall short too often.

Like all of us, if Dave keeps falling short and keeps missing out on reinforcement for his efforts, he'll soon fall out of

love with the game of training and that'd be such a shame. Take a few steps back, keep your rate of reinforcement high and relax in the knowledge that tomorrow's another day.

So, that's adolescence for you.

Thank you for sharing your concerns and thank you for being the type of owner willing to step up and help Dave through his 'discovery' phrase. It's not personal and when you come out the other side with a dog that STILL *loves* the opportunity to live and train with you, you're set up for life.

? CASTRATION

Hi Steve,

I'd love your thoughts on castration. Due to a family member's illness, we're soon to become the proud 'adoptive' parents of a beautiful cross-breed dog called Tommy. He's still only four months old, so it's a way off yet, but already everyone I speak to seems to have an opinion on castration, with the common phrase being that it's 'the responsible thing to do'. We'd never breed from him but surely I can prevent that without having to put him through castration? I appreciate that I have a 'male stick-together-lads' attitude to this and even as I write this letter I keep folding my legs ... however, surgery does seem drastic.

Can you point me in the right direction please?

Robert

Hi Robert,

I feel for you, it's a minefield out there and in addition to the question of 'to castrate or not' for males, I am also often asked 'to spay or not' for females. However, whereas each gender comes with their own suite of issues, as a dog trainer I am contacted far more frequently about my opinions on castration than spaying.

With Tommy, I wish I could give you a definite Yay or Nay and swiftly move on to a less gonadal arena, but I can't. My advice just can't be as simple as 'all in' or 'all out'. Such binary decisions are rarely simple.

Here's the deal: I myself live with five dogs of which two are male, one male's castrated and the other isn't. Both are rescue dogs. Spider, the Whippet, is by nature a pretty highly strung character and he certainly benefits from his testicles and the confidence his testosterone provides. I'm thankful he's not castrated.

Pablo, my Staffordshire Bull Terrier, also came to me from a rescue centre. However, unlike Spider, he had been castrated before we found each other. Pablo is the most confident, in-yer-face-gis-us-a-kiss gregarious life and soul of the party you're ever going to meet, of any species! He needs more testosterone-induced confidence like Sonic the Hedgehog needs more Red Bull. Pablo being castrated is fine by me.

It's 'horses for courses' on this one. All I can do is offer a few pros and cons, suggest you continue your research, very much consider the individual dog in front of you and don't rush in.

Disclaimer: I don't own a tweed jacket or mustard-coloured corduroy pants. I've never worn brogues and I can rarely be seen driving a sports car in the Yorkshire Dales, ergo, I am not a vet. For medical advice, I always recommend you refer to a qualified veterinary professional but in order to answer your question from my perspective, I've jotted down a few thoughts and considerations to hopefully steer you in the right direction.

Castration is the removal of both testes – the main protagonists of testosterone production in males. Testosterone regulates a number of processes in the male body and plays a key role in sexual development and characteristics. Contrary to popular belief, testosterone doesn't actually trigger behaviours; however, it can certainly add 'fuel to the fire' by increasing the chances of behaviours such as scent-marking and humping (dogs, people, cushions, bedding, thin air). Testosterone in an entire male can sometimes be suspected to increase the speed of arousal to specific triggers at a faster rate of knots than would be expected from a castrated male. In my experience, it can sometimes also make it difficult for an un-castrated, AKA entire male, to 'back down' from another entire male dog who's 'giving it large' down the park. That being said, the behaviours such as mounting, scent-marking or over-reactivity may *not* be related to testosterone at all, but may well be fuelled by anxiety, over-arousal or changes in the environment.

ONE MAN'S MEAT IS ANOTHER MAN'S POISON

Testosterone can certainly help increase and maintain a dog's confidence. This may be a chore if you own a dog that already forcibly struts his stuff with the air of a heavyweight champion and international playboy, but it certainly may be a blessing if you're the owner of a dog that needs all the help he can get to not be afraid of the world.

Anecdotally, I've seen many, many dogs in the past that feel the need to over-react aggressively in the presence of other dogs, *not* because they want to take on the world, but because they fear the other dogs and lack the confidence to react in any other way. The insecure dog who felt forced to react aggressively in the past to 'frighten off' the other dog may well have discovered that that particular behaviour 'works' for them, so the aggressive displays become reinforced, and therefore a more likely go-to coping mechanism in the future. So often these dogs have been castrated, and commonly far too young. I so wish I could've planted them back on so we could lean on that testosterone to give the dog more confidence in how to learn other, less stressful coping strategies such as avoidance, subtle body language and referring to their owner for support.

In my opinion, if the dog is showing any kind of fearful, timid, anxious or insecure behaviours, including aggression, then as far as I'm concerned that's a big tick in the box marked 'don't castrate' – at the very least until a good training schedule has helped you work through these issues and you've had a good 12 months of steady progress and no evidence of further fearful or aggressive events.

'Entire' dogs obviously have more of an eye for the ladies, so calling them back from female dogs or sassy doggy smells may be more of a challenge than with a castrated male. Although castration *may* help reduce some unwanted behaviours such as running away or aggression, you will also need to run a behaviour modification programme alongside any surgery as the unwanted behaviours that have happened in the past will now have a history of reinforcement. Surgery alone just won't cut it, as it were.

Although living with an adolescent dog can be a testing time (see page 242) – having to deal with the teenage problems of 'selective deafness', over-excitability and an awareness of their own sexual prowess developing – simply *picking their pockets* is not the answer. Nurse them through the adolescent period with safe, empathetic care and kind, positive training. When the dog is through adolescence and hits full maturity at approximately 18–24 months, then we can talk again.

The really good news is that now there's a 'try before you buy' option! 'Chemical castration' is becoming more popular, certainly as a first 'port of call', as it allows the owner to see the behavioural impact castration will actually have on the dog, without having to sign his testicles away forever and suffer any potential side effects. Chemical castration is performed by injecting a small implant into the back of the dog's neck which is gradually broken down by the dog's body, slowly releasing sustained levels of active ingredients which essentially control the testes in the male dog, reducing the level of testosterone produced. Implants generally last for six or 12 months. It should be noted that after implant, testosterone actually increases for the initial fortnight, and then drops at approximately four to six weeks after implantation to a level that mirrors predicted testosterone levels post-castration.

The idea is that during the period of implantation you will be able to see the potential behavioural effects that surgical castration would deliver, and the beauty of it is, you can repeat the implant process as many times as you like to ensure you make the right decision given all the information available. It's a popular route to take in Northern Europe with the implant simply being repeated for as long as required, whereas in the UK it tends to be used more as a one-off test-drive, a *teste-drive* if you will, to see if castration is the right decision or not. An implant may sound a little *Total Recall* but it's a great way to assess the potential benefits of castration (or not) without making an irreversible mistake. Many rescue centres in certain countries (although not all) will promote castration for all their male dogs to limit breeding and therefore, in theory, reduce the ever-growing burden of unwanted dogs on society. Rescue centres, vets, trainers, owners ... we'll all have different views due to our unique perspectives and I can certainly sympathise with the view of the heroes on the front line of rescue centres to castrate males to halt reproduction. I understand the motivation behind it, but flagging castration up as the broad-brush 'responsible thing to do', in my opinion just isn't that simple.

In the USA, many of the states require by law that any dog rehomed from a shelter be neutered, *regardless* of that dog's age, behaviour or temperament. That's just too damn carte blanche IMO. Neutering can affect a dog's body, potentially affect their health and often massively affect a dog's behaviour, which in turn will affect everyone in that dog's life. The decision to castrate needs to be from a study of one, considering the individual. It shouldn't be a corporate, non-negotiable policy.

In Norway, it used to actually be illegal to castrate a dog and only 7-8% of dogs in Sweden are neutered. Apparently, 80% of dogs in the USA are castrated. Stray dogs in Norway are not a problem; stray dogs in the USA are. Castration is certainly not a replacement for good training and a responsible owner.

If the motivation behind the surgery is purely to prevent reproduction, then to avoid negative health implications and to keep the production of testosterone intact, vasectomy is an option. Although not as commonplace as castration, it's worth having a chat with your vet about it as an alternative. Whereas castration tends to be a slightly bigger deal surgery-wise, a vasectomy is a relatively simple procedure as the testicles remain in situ and the sterilisation takes place by cutting, clamping or tying-off the *vas deferens*, who contrary to an answer given at my local pub quiz, is not a World Cup-winning Dutch footballer, but is in fact the duct that transports sperm from the testicles. Vasectomy is not a 'go-to' for most practices, but it's definitely worth discussing with your vet.

So, there you have it. Without meeting you and your dog to discuss their particular behaviour and character, I can't be more specific but, as I've outlined, there are options available to you now that will help prevent you from making a regrettable snap decision. So continue to gather evidence, look after your dog, talk to the pros and take your time.

THE USE OF FOOD
IN TRAINING

Hi Steve,

I think you may well be named in our divorce papers! I'm
making great progress following your tips in Easy Peasy
Puppy Squeezy, but my husband, who really wants to
get involved in the training, says he doesn't believe in
using food. Please either give me some tips as to how
to negotiate with him, or give me the number of a good
solicitor!

Patti

Hi Patti!

Ah, the age-old '*don't believe*'. Why is it that toys are accepted, petting and praise are accepted, but the use of food as a reinforcer often needs some form of *belief* system, like it's a religion or some weird cult? Empirical evidence should be enough and there's plenty of that around us.

The objection to using food is never based on its success, without doubt it's an amazing tool for fast, effective animal training. Nobody marks the sea mammal trainer down for feeding the dolphin a mackerel for the desired result or the bird of prey handler for feeding the kestrel a slither of meat for flying to the glove. So why on earth do people criticise dog trainers for the same?

Firstly, I want to list a few considerations below, and then I'll Q&A a few of the more common food objections. Hopefully you can find some ammunition here to help clarify the bone of contention for your husband!

- Don't confuse effective dog training with love. No one admits it, but I think some people think that if they use food for training the dog won't love, or even worse, respect them enough. 'Love' and 'receiving food' are not mutually exclusive, in fact, quite the opposite!

🐾 If you had only 10 days to teach your dog a behaviour that will save his life in a situation due to happen on the eleventh day, would you want to have treats available for you to help train that behaviour?

🐾 On a scale of 1 to 10, how much does your dog love their food?

  On a scale of 1 to 10, how much do you want your dog to enjoy their training with you? (If your answer is anything less that 10, you're a sociopath!)

🐾 When anyone asks me to do something, unless they're bullying me, I'd like to know 'why?' If I understand the 'why' and I understand the *benefit* to me, I'll do my best to comply with the request.

  Same with dogs.

🐾 The behaviours we all do are essentially driven to get something pleasant, or avoid something nasty. If I get something pleasant for doing a behaviour, I'm keen to do it again and again, which builds fluency and consistency.

  If I get something nasty for doing a behaviour, or for not doing a behaviour, I'll look to avoid it. No fluency, no consistency.

- If you want a gold medal (for a dog, that's often food), and you only get a silver medal (for a dog, that's often praise), it's disappointing, demoralising even. But if you give food *and* praise, the praise is elevated.

Let's now have a look at the common objections to using food and how we can shift perspectives:

- **Objection**: I don't want to use food as the dog will only do it if I have food in my hand.
  Answer: YES! I completely agree. When used *incorrectly*, it's extremely limiting, that's why we're going to use it correctly!

It's important in animal training that as much as possible, and as soon as possible, food is produced and presented *after* the behaviour, not *before*. The only exception is times when we need to initially *lure* the behaviour, such as for our Chin Rest exercise (see page 37) or for the early luring stages of various Tricks (see page 151).

It's not just food, but all reinforcers need to come as a consequence of the behaviour, to make the behaviour more likely to reoccur. *Consequences* come *after* a behaviour, never *before*.

If food is continuously presented *before* the behaviour, then the food becomes part of the cue. That's a slippery slope because in the future if the cue (the food) isn't presented, then the behaviour will be absent too. Trained *incorrectly*, you can bet your bottom dollar the dog will only do it if there's food in your hand!

At the park I can always tell the people that have used food incorrectly in their training. It's evident that they've used food as part of the cue (pre-behaviour) rather than the consequence (post-behaviour) because they stand at the gate and shout...

'Come!' (dog does nothing)...

Again, 'Come! (dog does nothing)...

Then they *put their hand in their pocket, produce the food* and shout ... 'Sausages!' and the dog recalls like a missile!

They've taught their dog that the cue to do a recall isn't 'Come!' but is the action of their owner putting their hand in their pocket and producing a treat.

Dogs are nothing but fair. They do what we teach them to do.

It's consequences that makes behaviour reliable.
Use food as a consequence, not as a cue.

> ❧ **Objection:** It's wrong to have to bribe the dog to do something.
>
> **Answer:** YES! Again, we can agree. Food used as part of the cue, *prior* to the behaviour is a bribe.
>
> Food used as part of the consequence, *after* the behaviour is using it (correctly!) as a reinforcer.

* **Objection**: I don't want to have to give the dog a treat every single time I ask the dog to do something.
  Answer: Uncanny, AGAIN, I agree! (See Life Rewards pages 224–30)

* **Objection**: The dog should do it for *me* out of respect, not for the food.
  Answer: Why? You're not Tarzan! The word 'respect' is a bit of an icky one when used in dog training. What do people mean when they say they want their dog to 'respect' them? It can mean one of two things: fear them or do what they're told to do.

  Use punishment if you want the dog to fear you.

  Use reinforcement if you want the dog to do what they're told to do.

  Respect doesn't come in to it.

  If you crave respect, be a Goodfella.

* **Objection**: Using food all the time will make my dog fat.
  Answer: Yes! Yes, it will! If ... the dog is eating more calories than they're burning. Adjust their meal intake and/or adjust their exercise so they benefit from a fantastic training tool AND they stay healthy. Easy Peasy!

🐾 **Objection**: My dog won't take food outside of the house.

Answer: Sometimes owners tell me that their dog won't eat out on walks so they don't use food for training, instead they resort to trying to use toys to reinforce the behaviours they want. Although using toys at certain stages of training and for particular exercises can be an awesome way to reinforce behaviours, especially when you want more speed and urgency, sometimes that additional injection of chase/grab/bite/adrenalin while out on a walk isn't the healthiest cocktail for the dog to associate and expect in certain environments and situations.

We need to put the horse before the cart here and ask why the dog won't, or even *can't*, accept food in this environment. Very often it's because the dog is far too heightened to take food in such environments; if the dog's fight-or-flight sympathetic part of the nervous system is on standby, the body may need to reject food as it potentially will have far more important matters to funnel its energy towards. Remember, how the dog feels comes first, the behaviours come second. If the dog doesn't feel comfortable enough in a particular environment to take food as reinforcement for an exercise, then we need to swallow our pride and teach the exercise in a less distracting, 'safer' environment first, then as confidence and security grows, shift through the gears with a view to steadily maintaining the same behaviour but in increasingly distracting environments.

If for some reason, you *must* take your dog to an environment where they're too aroused to take food, don't add pressure by trying to train and offer impotent reinforcers – you'll become an annoyance, the training will be duff and future sessions will be 'poisoned'. Simply sit, keep your dog safe, let them know you've got their back and at least help desensitise them to the location. Over time they'll be able to relax, be able to take food, and then you'll be back in business!

Dale Carnegie, the famous salesman and self-help guru, said, 'The only way to motivate someone is to find out what they want, and then show them how to get it.' I always ask my clients what behaviour they want from their dog and I show them how to get it. While we're at it, we also ask the dog what THEY want and we show THEM how to get it!

Finally, I used to be employed as a training consultant for various security dog handling companies and, of course, I was seen by many as a sissy, tree-hugging, cookie-chucking 'softie' dog trainer.

'It's all very well training Jack Russells that way, but it won't work for Rottweilers.' (As if tall kids need to be taught differently in school to the shorter ones.) My favourite reply to a macho He-man dog handler when he told me he didn't 'believe' in using food was, 'I understand. What's your FEAR of using food?' He couldn't grab the treat bag quick enough to demonstrate he wasn't afraid of using food! Once he started to get results, the rest was history.

I'm sorry to say that in my experience the 'What's your fear of using food?' only works with men and their hair-trigger egos but who knows, with your husband it may well be your get out of jail card!

Good luck!

P.S. Treatit & Repeatit, London, K9 6OG

DOG CLASSES

Hi Steve,

We're the proud owners of a very bouncy puppy German Shepherd called King who we've just welcomed into our home only a few days ago. He's settled in well at home with us but we want to get him into classes ASAP so he can learn what we expect of him and to teach him some manners. I know King needs to realise we're the pack leader, so we need to eat before him, go through doorways first, not let him upstairs or on to furniture, etc. The last dog training classes I went to were over 20 years ago, but I'd love to know what else I need to look out for when searching for appropriate classes.

Best,
Malcolm

Hi Malcolm,

Thanks a million for your mail: brace yourself my friend!

Life's going to be so much easier for both you and King if we reframe the enquiry for you. To paraphrase John F. Kennedy, it's not a question of what you can 'expect of King, but what King can expect of you!' When you go to a training school with King, he can expect you to keep him safe. *That means you don't go anywhere that uses harsh methods or equipment.*

When you ask King to come to you, or to sit, he can expect to receive something pleasant in exchange. Something that will encourage him to offer the behaviour for you again. *That means you need to go to a school that focuses on positive reinforcement.*

As for pack leader, to paraphrase another great American, Al Pacino, 'Forget about it!' The pack leader ethos is an old approach that really doesn't serve in improving training or building relationships. It's kinda sexy to some, but it just doesn't hold water. No one wants to hear their dog is not coming back when called because the dog hasn't been taught the benefits of a recall, they'd rather hear the dog isn't coming back because he's 'dominant'. That way it's the dog's fault. Nope, I'm not having it. It's never the dog's fault.

This pack leader / hierarchy / dominance idea came about many, many years ago following a study of wolf packs kept in captivity. Unfortunately, certain dog trainers of the time put two and two together, and came up with a lemon.

I don't want you to think I'm being mean here because it's true that the only thing two dog trainers will agree on is that the third one is doing it wrong, but when it's damaging to the dog and owner's quality of life, I've got to speak up.

The theory of 'eat before your dog' came about because it was thought that 'in the wild' (an impotent precursor to any statement discussing domestic dog training), the dominant animal eats before the subservient. As a kid, I remember attending a dog training presentation at a school fête where they made the statement that the pack leader must always eat first. They then went on to demonstrate a down with an audience member's dog, and gave a treat to the dog when they did so. I innocently (honestly!) put my hand up to ask why the trainer didn't feel the need to eat before giving the dog the food. The reply? 'I'll get to that later.' Over 40 years later, I've been checking my post for a reply … nothing!

The theory of 'going through doorways before your dog' is an old chestnut that harks back to the premise that 'when wolves go hunting, they walk in single file with the alpha at the front'. Again, even if we were to turn a blind eye to the whole 'different animals' issue, wolves don't hunt in single file like some blood-thirsty cycling pursuit team. They spread out, searching, then surrounding their prey. Dogs go through doorways first not because they're trying to dominate us, but because they're curious, enthusiastic and they move faster than us two-legged sloths! Do those trainers that subscribe to this really go through every door before their dog? At night-time when they're letting their dogs out the back door for a final wee in the rain? Really?

I used to often go out walking through the fields with several rescue dogs. There'd be me, always a German Shepherd, a few Labradors, perhaps a Springer and no doubt a Terrier or two. We used to walk from field to field to field. Whenever we got to a gate or stile it was never, 'Right, German Shepherd first, then the Lab ... Terrier? You can sod off to the back!' The dogs never bothered with who goes through first, I figured neither should I, then. They're the experts!

When I was 19, I was handling a security dog and was called to a potential break-in at a warehouse. Did I want to go through each doorway before my dog? Nope! If it doesn't make sense to me, I don't do it. And nor should you. And nor should your dog. And if you ever get a wolf ... well, we can cross that bridge when we come to it!

The final point you're making is not allowing the dog upstairs or on the furniture. That's fine if the reason is because you want to keep your sofa clean or just want upstairs to be a dog-free zone. However, don't restrict yourself to that if the reasoning is purely because a dog trainer told you that to allow it would cause 'dominance issues'. It won't.

The theory of not allowing the dog on the furniture or upstairs skew-wiffidely stems from the 'pack-leaders choosing to sleep on the high areas of the den for comfort, security and hierarchal reasons'. Again, don't sweat it: different species, different rules. Dogs don't aim to get up high on platforms to dominate us. (That's cats, they definitely do that!) Each to their own, but I personally love having my dogs up on the couch with me watching TV. Living with dogs is a team game, not a battle for supremacy. If height was gained in order to dominate, we'd all be serving the Bird Gods.

The ethos of all dog training principles should be you working *with* your dog. If it ever feels like it's you *versus* your dog, we're in bother. With all the above in mind, let's focus on what you *should* be looking out for in a good dog training class:

- Word of mouth is great, but even assassins get business through recommendations! Search for a trainer that's qualified with a body such as my organisation, the Institute of Modern Dog Trainers. That way you can be confident of a strong code of ethics as well as a trainer that has undergone a rigorous assessment process to ensure they can walk the walk.

Don't be shy of going along to a class or two to observe without King. The class should feel comfortable and relaxed, no more than six to eight dogs per trainer and the general vibe should be chilled and friendly. No jerks (in the verb or the noun sense), no shouting, nothing that feels stressy. The dogs, owners and trainer should all seem to be enjoying each other's company. Check: do all the dogs look happy? Do all the owners? You should be witnessing owners that are invested, happy and comfortable enough to ask questions. If the only talking is coming from the person who's the trainer, then that person is not actually training the class, they're merely stewarding. It needs to be a two-way street. Scratch that, it needs to be a three-way street.

I hope that helps, I think it may have sounded a little preachy. I didn't mean to, it's only because I love you! I wholeheartedly believe that going to a good dog training school can help you and King really get the most out of each other, so do your research, find a good positive dog trainer and don't worry about pack-leader-hierarchy-dominance stuff.

If they wanted to take over, believe me, we're wide open – they would've done so by now!

CANINE COGNITIVE DYSFUNCTION

Hi Steve,

I hope you can help. Over the last few weeks we've noticed our 12-year-old German Shepherd Dotty doing a few odd little behaviours around the house. Nothing dramatic, little things like barking at 'nothing', or certainly nothing I can see, pacing and seemingly being a bit more stubborn with her responses to exercises I <u>know</u> she knows.

I appreciate she's not the young gun-ho 'working' dog she used to be, but this apparent disobedience seems a bit sudden. (We still love her dearly though!)

I spoke with the dog trainer we used to go to and they mentioned it could just be old age or a condition called Canine Cognitive Dysfunction, but couldn't tell me much more, so I don't know if it's a training or medical issue. Do I need a behaviourist or a vet?

What can you tell me?

Babs

Hi Babs (seems so familiar!),

Canine Cognitive Dysfunction: although not a training or behavioural issue, CCD is often confused by owners as such, hence the reason I want to put my head above the parapet to discuss it a little further for you.

I dedicate my life to dogs for the simple reason that I *know* they dedicate their lives to us. If our dogs live to a ripe old age, as I hope they do, there's a very good chance they're going to need a little extra support and understanding from us to make their fourth act as comfortable and stress-free as possible. As our dogs age, elements of CCD are a common occurrence and, as forewarned is forearmed, I want to offer an overview of what CCD is, plus make a few little suggestions that could be a big help.

CCD is a term used to describe the changes seen in many ageing dogs due to mental decline. Like most neurological conditions CCD comes hand-in-hand with behavioural changes that can be at best confusing, at worse upsetting.

Knowledge is power, however, and the more we can understand and prepare then the less we're going to feel helpless when the time comes.

Like all medical conditions it's always best to consult your vet as soon as you suspect any issues and in fact, as we all get older, we're more likely to suffer some deterioration (Alright Grandad!), so a diarised vet visit at least every six months will certainly help you and your vet keep your dog as comfortable as possible. The more familiar your vet is with your ageing dog, the sooner they'll notice any changes and the sooner they can act.

Signs of CCD can be seen from the age of eight onwards (sometimes sooner in giant breeds) and the symptoms can slowly multiply as your dog progresses from mild through to stronger behavioural changes. I've listed some of the signs below.

I think it'll be prudent if you can tick all off the observable signs you suspect Dotty is already presenting, that way you and your vet will be able to understand what stage she's at and therefore be best equipped as to how to help her:

- Shifts in sleep pattern
- Changes in interactions with family members
- Pacing
- Circling
- Loss of toilet-training
- Previous training cues forgotten
- Disorientation
- Getting stuck under furniture
- Staring into the distance for no apparent reason
- Restlessness
- Barking throughout the night

- 🐾 Getting trapped in the corner of a room
- 🐾 Difficulty with eating or drinking, e.g. inaccurate with mouth or can't find the bowl
- 🐾 Not responding to name
- 🐾 Easy to startle
- 🐾 Noise sensitivity.

When you tick off some of the behavioural changes listed above, it'll be important that you and your vet run through a process of 'rule-outs', which is another way of asking, 'Yes, it could be a symptom of CCD, but what else could it be a symptom of instead of CCD?'

For example:

Difficulty with eating: could be a sore tooth.

Not responding to name: could be deafness.

Restlessness: may be sore hips when she lies downs.

Noise sensitivity: maybe a door slammed, causing her to tense up, which in turn caused pain in her sore hips. She associates the noise of the door with the pain, causing her to become sensitised to the sound of the door or other noises.

Rule-outs are an essential route to the diagnosis of medical issues AND behavioural issues.

Although to date there is no *cure* for CCD, there are certainly many ways that you and your vet can add benefit and perhaps limit the progression of the condition. For example, some prescribed drugs can slow down the process by increasing blood flow and chemical messages to the brain. Your vet may also be able to recommend dietary changes such as added fatty acids, minerals and vitamins to increase mental alertness.

You yourself can weigh-in to help with some of the actions below:

Routine and Familiarity

* Keep everything as routine as possible. Older dogs, and people for that matter, like routine: toilet breaks, exercise, naps, champagne at weddings, sherry at Christmas, etc!

  Try and keep the layout of house and garden furniture the same, with a few safety exceptions if necessary, as listed on the next page.

* Manage unfamiliar visitors to your house.

* Keep evening, bedtime, feeding, exercise and toileting routines as clockwork as possible.

* If need be, revert back to a toilet training routine as described in *Easy Peasy Puppy Squeezy* to limit accidents.

Safety

- Puppy-proof your house all over again. The circle of life and all that!

- Remove the risk of trip hazards or falling off steps from the house and garden.

- Be aware of loose cables should your dog find their way behind furniture.

- Consider moving water and feeding bowls to the corner of the room to help Dotty locate them and to prevent her from walking through them.

- Put mats down on potentially slippery surfaces such as wooden or polished floors.

- Protect from over-exuberant or unfamiliar dogs when outside. If Dotty has any aches and pains, we certainly don't want those aggravated, or pain being associated with the presence of 'other dogs'. We definitely don't want her to associate 'being outside' with pain. In addition, Dotty's body language, sight or hearing may not be as on point as it used to be and we don't want her communication to be misinterpreted. We don't want the other dog getting the wrong end of the stick, as it were.

Enrichment

Mental and physical enrichment have continuously been shown to prevent and slow down the onset of CCD:

- Physical health permitting, make sure you keep up with regular walks at routine times to allow Dotty to explore, sniff and watch the world go by. Keep the fires of curiosity burning and remember it's not about distance, it's about finding, enjoying and exercising that curiosity muscle that all dogs are born with. Due to age, frequent shorter walks throughout the day may suit better rather than one long slog.

- Play with your dog! Cuddles, 'competition' over a tea towel, flicking treats to pounce onto. This time is golden, make the most of it.

- Offer activities that provide the opportunity for Dotty to stretch and exercise all of her senses: smell, sight, sound and touch. A rucksack walk will gently manipulate all of these areas for you without the risk of over-exertion (see page 208).

  Or simply scatter Dotty's food in the garden like a trail of breadcrumbs for her to follow and eat, so she can joyfully re-live her predatory prowess.

Getting old is not the end of the world. If we're lucky, we get to share a long and happy life with our dogs. Ageing is part of the process and it's only fair that we put as much thought and effort into preparing to live with an older dog as we do when prepping for a puppy. Our old dogs were pups once too, and I've always felt that old dogs are special, they're worldly wise and they're beautiful. How wonderful for a dog to experience a life of living for nothing but joy – we can offer that, from beginning to end. There's nothing I wouldn't give for another 20 minutes sat outside watching the world go by with my arm around my old German Shepherd Alfa.

Living with an older dog isn't a hardship, it's a gift and you're lucky to be in a position to make the most of it.

Enjoy it, for me ... and for Alfa.

A FEW CLOSING WORDS

So, now it's time for me to hand the lead back over to you. You've got this!

Take everything one step at a time and remember to celebrate each and every success along the way. It's so much more than 'training'. It's creating a bond, it's being able to help each other through the tough times and it's about living your best life with your best friend.

The responsibility is ours to teach our dogs the necessary life skills to help them negotiate our human world, to show them the behaviours that pay the best dividends and to continue to allow them to be the most optimistic characters possible.

Remember, there's no such thing as a 'fail' in dog training, it's only ever just information. If you hit a wall, simply lower your expectations, train at an achievable level, hit your target and move on.

I don't want to talk myself out of job here but some days, you just won't fancy doing any formal training, and that's just fine. Dog training isn't against the clock; if your time with your dog is better spent sitting out in the back garden in the sun, stroking their belly as they look into your eyes and can't believe how lucky they are to be with you, then ... ace! You may not be *training*, but your dog will certainly be *learning*. They'll be learning that you're pretty cool to hang out with, that they feel good when they're next to you and that they love your company. Pretty good foundations for recall, loose lead walking and everything else in between, I'd say!

Quality beats quantity every time and the fact is: **training dogs is always a work in progress.**

If you follow the *Easy Peasy* way and use positive, ethical and stress-free methods, you'll never stop training, and your dog will never want you to.

My own special rescue dog Pablo came to me with every problem under the sun, including many of the issues discussed here, but it was by working through his problems, teaching him that he's allowed to trust people again and by giving him the confidence to try new behaviours, even if he didn't succeed every time, that he learned to live his life to the full again. He's a joy to live with and always brings a smile or affectionate lick to the face of anyone he meets.

We all think we live with the best dog ... and we're all correct.

ACKNOWLEDGEMENTS

Thank you to my dogs, who made me write this book and thank you to your dogs, who made you buy it. Thanks to Matthew Phillips at Blink who magically encouraged me to write more words, and to Martin Roach who magically put them in the right order.

Shout out to John Kavanagh, a coach after my own heart. I tip my hat to you with 'advanced is simply the basics done well'.

As always, thank you from the bottom of my heart to anyone that makes the lives of dogs better. Thank you to Emilia Clarke for her kind words on the cover. (Now get on with your homework!) High-five to Gina and Luke who, I assume, really, really appreciated my phenomenal singing as I wrote ... and in case I never get another chance, thank you John, Paul, George and Ringo.

INDEX

EVEN MORE FROM
STEVE MANN

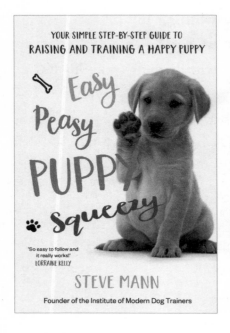

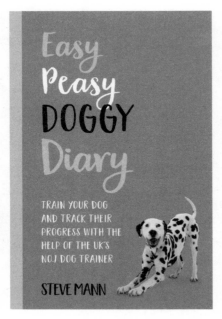

Easy Peasy Puppy Squeezy is the puppy training book you've been waiting for! It really is easy peasy and every tip, trick and lesson will bring you and your puppy closer together.

Record your dog's journey and learn extra techniques with *Easy Peasy Doggy Diary*.

'So easy to follow and it really works!'
LORRAINE KELLY

'Dog Training Genius!'
EMILIA CLARKE